ARMING THE STATE

ARMING THE STATE

Military Conscription in the Middle East and Central Asia 1775–1925

Edited by

ERIK J. ZÜRCHER

I.B.Tauris *Publishers*
LONDON ● NEW YORK

Published in 1999 by I.B.Tauris & Co Ltd
Victoria House, Bloomsbury Square, London WC1B 4DZ
175 Fifth Avenue, New York NY 10010
Website: http://www.ibtauris.com

In the United States and Canada distributed by St. Martin's Press
175 Fifth Avenue, New York NY 10010

ISBN 1 86064 404 X

A full CIP record for this book is available from the British Library
A full CIP record for this book is available from the Library of Congress

Library of Congress catalog card: available

Typeset in 10/12pt Ehrhardt by the Midlands Book Typesetting Company,
Loughborough
Printed and bound in Great Britain by WBC Ltd, Bridgend

Contents

Acknowledgement

The chapters in this collection were presented as papers during a symposium organized jointly by the International Institute of Social History and the Middle East Institute of the University of Nijmegen, on the occasion of the latter's fiftieth anniversary. The symposium was held in Nijmegen on 2–3 October 1997. The editor wishes to thank the organizers in Nijmegen for their generous hospitality.

Four of the chapters in this volume were published in a slightly different form in *International Review of Social History* 43 (1998). They are reproduced here with the kind permission of the editors.

Introduction: Conscription and Resistance. The Historical Context

Jan Lucassen and Erik Jan Zürcher

The options of the state: military recruitment systems

For most of the nineteenth and twentieth centuries, universal conscription has been by far the predominant system of military recruitment, but the phenomenon has received surprisingly little attention from social historians.[1] This lack of attention is all the more surprising if one considers the interesting position occupied by conscription at the crossroads of wage- and non-wage labour and free and unfree labour.

This collection deals with the spread of the conscription system mainly in one specific area (the Middle East), where it has been the most prominent feature of the establishment of increased and centralized state control over societies which until relatively recent times consisted of largely self-sufficient agrarian communities with very little contact with the outside world. The introduction of universal conscription faced both states and populations with entirely new demands and problems.

In order to understand the specific characteristics of the system, a comparative approach is necessary, placing it in the context of two repertoires: that of the options facing states in search of military resources and that of the options open to individuals, communities and entire societies defending their interests in the face of the demands made by the state. Conscription is, after all, only one form of recruitment of soldiers, feasible and desirable only under a specific set of conditions, so to be understood it has to be studied within the framework of military recruitment through the ages.

In adopting this comparative approach, we aim to draw attention to the similarities between the developments in Europe and in the Middle East, thus bringing out the dynamics inherent in different systems and, incidentally, contributing to the struggle against orientalism and its essentialist division of the world into 'civilizations'.[2]

A useful way of addressing this problem is by making use of the model proposed by Charles Tilly regarding state-building through war and state monopolization of violence.[3] This implies a continuous rejuvenation of the state, including its armed forces, not simply or solely as a reaction to outside threats, but as a response to continuous changes in the availability of resources.

In the Tilly model, the tax-raising potential of a state determines the choice of a particular recruitment system and consequently for the possibilities of resistance. We shall therefore make a distinction between the situations where taxation is not an option and those where it is, especially in the towns. In the latter case, a division of labour may occur between towns with essentially defensive militias and the much more mobile and offensive army of the state. With the help of the money raised through taxation, the state has a choice of three strategies: recruitment of unfree men (subjects, subjugated or purchased) who may or may not be paid; recruitment in exchange for wages on the national or international labour market; and recruitment of free subjects, who are fed and clothed, but not paid anything like a normal wage. In this last strategy, the free subjects may be volunteers or they may be conscripts – in which case their freedom is obviously severely limited.

We will now attempt a brief overview, a catalogue, of forms of recruitment employed in the Islamic Middle East, set against the background of developments in Europe in the early-modern and modern periods.

Forms of recruitment

Taking as point of departure the state's ability to raise taxes for military purposes, we may discern four major types of recruitment of men for the army and navy in the Middle East and Europe between the late seventeenth and early twentieth centuries: feudal recruitment, unfree recruitment, recruitment on the labour market and conscription.

Feudal military mobilization

This system was based primarily on the non-monetary relation between the state (for example, king or sultan) and feudal lords or tribal chiefs. In return for autogestion, land or property rights or tax-exemption, these lords undertook to provide soldiers.[4] The soldiers fought under their own commanders, with their own armour and/or horses and were mostly stationed locally. In the period under discussion, this system was most common in the borderlands where the settled parts of Eurasia meet the steppes and deserts.

The question whether the Ottoman Empire knew true feudalism has been debated fiercely,[5] but the empire's *timar* system, which gave members of the cavalry (*sipahi*s) usufruct of state lands in exchange for military service, certainly had common features with the feudal system, even if the relatively strong Ottoman state, its monopoly of cereal trade and its support for the rights of peasants meant that the Ottoman 'gentry' always enjoyed less freedom than its European counterpart. The *sipahi* contingents' freedom of action was also curtailed because during the campaigning season they were not stationed locally, but formed part of the imperial army. The system was never employed throughout the Sultan's domains. It was one of the main instruments for recruitment in the central provinces (Anatolia and the Balkans) until the late seventeenth century by which time it had grown obsolete in two senses: as a medieval technology confronting gunpowder armies, and as a means of raising money at a time when the state was desperate for cash income.[6]

Systems which cannot be called feudal, but which nevertheless involved service in exchange for non-monetary rewards, are those that involved armed peasants (*Wehrbauern*) such as the Cossacks in the Russian Empire. A system which might be considered as falling into this category was the recruitment of *levend*s by the Ottoman Empire in the seventeenth and eighteenth centuries. While these were partly drawn from the 'town riff-raff', many of them came from villages which were granted tax exemptions in exchange for service. When its traditional core forces became less and less useful, the empire, in spite of its ideological attachment to the concept of a sharp division between an armed governing elite (*askeri*) and unarmed productive subjects (*reaya*), came to rely heavily on these troops.

Tribal forces of course lost their importance in the main countries of Europe very early on. The defeat of the Jacobite Scottish clans in the campaign of 1745 could be regarded as their last stand, unless one regards the social organization of the Cossacks as 'tribal'. Although the Ottoman Empire did use tribal forces, they were never central to its military organization, being auxiliaries of often rather doubtful value. In Persia on the other hand, as Stephanie Cronin shows in Chapter 9, tribal forces made up the backbone of the army until well into the twentieth century. When forces modelled on the Russian Cossacks were formed in the Ottoman Empire and Iran in the late nineteenth century, they were in both cases recruited from among the tribes.

Unfree recruitment

This system is based on the relation between the state and its unfree subjects, on conquest and subjugation,[7] or on trade in the international slave market. According to the different character of the unfree status we can identify four types:

Conscription of serfs in Russia[8]

Under Peter the Great the Russian Empire abandoned free recruitment and drafted subjects – nearly always serfs – for no less than lifetime service. Those who had to leave their villages for ever were usually designated by the village community, the *mir*. Serfs could also be condemned to military service by their feudal lords or by the courts. In 1793 the period of service was reduced to twenty-five years, but given the low life expectancy at the time this made very little difference in practice. In 1834 the term of service was reduced to a de facto twelve years and in 1855 to ten. In 1874 universal conscription on the modern pattern was introduced, an innovation made possible only by the abolition of serfdom in 1861.

The press-gang

The roughest and least regulated of the systems of unfree recruitment was that of the 'press', under which able bodied men were simply rounded up and requisitioned for army or navy. It is documented for several navies, the British and Ottoman (who used it in the Greek archipelago) among them, in the seventeenth and eighteenth centuries, but seems to have been used in wartime emergencies rather than as a regular instrument of recruitment.[9]

Military slavery

Military slavery was widely used in the whole Middle East from the ninth century until the nineteenth. It has been said that the use of slave armies was inherent in Islamic organization,[10] but if we take into account the widespread use of unfree enrolment outside the Muslim world, this conclusion seems doubtful. Rather, it seems that the *form* of enslavement, not enslavement as such, was traditional in this part of the world. Broadly speaking, two types of slave army were employed in the Islamic world. The older one, for which the term 'Mamluk' is used, was made up of well-paid professional soldiers who had been bought or captured outside the Islamic world, primarily in the Turkic steppes or in the Caucasus. The other, newer, system was that employed by the Ottomans from the late fourteenth century onwards, under which boys from Christian peasant families in the Balkans and Anatolia were enslaved and recruited for the Janissary corps (from *Yeni Çeri* – New Army).[11] In both cases the logic of the system seems to have been that people were recruited from among those furthest removed from the establishment[12] (although, of course, in both cases the slave soldiers developed into a power elite themselves).

Slaves in the navy

Convicts and slaves were used, primarily on the Mediterranean galleys,[13] by all powers until well into the eighteenth century, when sailing-ships had made galleys obsolete as a fighting force. For example, at the battle of Lepanto (1571) all the fleets were heavily dependent on Greek, Albanian, Bosnian and other slaves from the Balkans.[14] Outside the Mediterranean, the Portuguese seem to have used slaves on their sailing ships, as the Dutch did occasionally on their East Indiamen.[15] The Ottoman navy used slave power as much as the European states, but Panzac's research indicates that it later became less dependent on it than its Christian adversaries.

Recruitment on the labour market

This system was based on the relation between the state and the (national or international) labour market. Remuneration took the form of wages or prize-money, booty or less directly material gains such as secular or religious honour.[16] Two ways of hiring soldiers were possible: either individual and direct recruitment or collective and indirect recruitment. As in all crafts and professions, some regions or ethnic communities specialized in this trade, as the following examples make clear.

Individual

Individual recruitment of mercenaries was employed by many great powers in Europe from the Middle Ages onwards. The recruits could be local but, especially wartime, they could come from far away. In the early-modern period the Venetians, the Spanish, the French, the Dutch and – after the 'Glorious Revolution' of 1689 – also the English used mercenaries. Irish, Scots, Swiss and inhabitants of some German states (for example, Hesse, Hannover and Brunswick) specialised in this trade. Their religious convictions could influence their attractiveness to foreign employers.[17]

An international maritime labour market, also involving the navies, seems to have come into being later. In the early-modern period only the Dutch Republic could really boast of having established one; followed only from the mid-nineteenth century by the Americans and then the British. Over the twentieth century a global maritime labour market was established, but by then it had lost its significance for the navies. In the Ottoman Empire we can also discern certain ethnic groups which specialized in this military trade, notably Albanians and Bosnians. Whatever their legal status and mode of payment, by the eighteenth century they were to all intents and purposes hired mercenaries. A man like the Albanian Mehmed Ali Pasha, whose army is the subject of Khaled Fahmy's chapter, can definitely be described as a successful soldier of fortune, as can the Bosnian Pasha of Acre, Jazzâr, who plays a prominent role in Dick Douwes's discussion of the Syrian situation (Chapter 8).

Collective

Group recruitment with the help of intermediaries was also common. It is not always possible to make a clear distinction between this form and individual recruitment, but in the cases of subsidy regiments and privateers, the form is mostly collective. The employment of privateers – essentially pirates sailing for booty under legal sanction by a state – continued until the 1850s in both the Christian and the Muslim worlds.[18] In the Ottoman case, the best-known example is that of the corsairs from the Barbary coast (Algiers, Tunis, Tripolitania and Cyrenaica), who in their turn employed free locals (Arabs and Turks) and slaves (including captured Christians). Outside Ottoman jurisdiction, the privateers of Salé and Tangiers earned a reputation as merciless hunters of the sea;[19] a well-known example from the Christian side is that of the Maltese. The equivalent of these naval mercenaries on land was the 'Uskoks' on the Ottoman–Austrian border, who at different times fought on both sides.[20] The Ottomans also used locally hired mercenaries on the Danube.

Beduin tribal forces were nearly always free actors, who were paid collectively for their services (although it has to be said that they were often paid for *not* attacking the Ottomans' own caravan trade, rather than for fighting in the sultan's cause).[21]

As all these examples make clear, different systems nearly always coexisted within one state. There was no clear-cut development from a 'primitive' to a 'modern' system through well-established intermediate stages.

Conscription, universal and otherwise

We now come to the main topic of this book: recruitment through conscription. Although essentially a modern system with its roots in the French revolutionary period, the phenomenon has predecessors in Medieval and early modern Europe. In order to understand the novelty of the system, we have first of all to make a distinction between indirect and direct conscription.

Indirect conscription

Before national, centralized and theoretically universal conscription was introduced, we can already discern older systems of indirect conscription which share some of its characteristics.[22] Peter the Great's conscript army was recruited indirectly in that the great landowners were charged with filling their complement of recruits and largely left free in their choice of conscripts. The actual selection was then mostly left to the village elders in the *mir*. The *bunichah* system introduced in Persia in the 1840s (and described by Cronin) was also of this type.

In most of Europe, from the Middle Ages onwards, we see local militia systems, mostly organized separately in the towns and in the countryside. In medieval and early-modern European towns craft guilds often provided a number of civic tasks such as fire-fighting and local defence. In the Dutch Republic more specialized militias (*schutterijen*) took over the task of defence, while in Venice craft guilds even had offensive duties when they had to take their turn at manning the galleys.[23] The countryside also often had militias for self-defence.[24] Villagers were often loosely organised and ill-trained, but the aptitudes which enabled them to survive in harsh circumstances gave them a natural ability as soldiers, especially in remote and mountainous areas.

In the pre-modern Middle East, towns had never achieved the corporate identity and autonomy which became the norm in late-medieval Europe. Middle Eastern states did not recognize the rights of 'citizens' (an alien concept in itself) to arm and defend themselves. Nevertheless, something approaching a town militia came into being when the Janissary army lost its original standing, professional and celibate character in the late sixteenth century. In the seventeenth and eighteenth centuries the corps developed close links with the craft guilds and in effect became a part-time militia of shopowners, ready to defend their interests against encroachments on the part of the state, but almost useless as an intrument of that state in warfare. Indeed, as Virginia Aksan describes in Chapter 2, finding alternatives to the Janissaries became a prime concern of the Ottoman government.

In spite of the theoretical monopolization of violence on the part of the state, the Ottoman (but also the Persian) countryside was quite heavily armed. The Ottoman state made use of this state of affairs when it began to recruit large numbers of young armed peasants as *levend*s in the seventeenth century and, as Douwes points out, in the nineteenth century disarming the countryside was as much a cause for resistance as the introduction of universal conscription.

Direct conscription

Direct conscription systems depend on the relation between the state and its individual free subjects. In most cases, remuneration only exists in the form of subsistance, although the state is responsible for clothing and equipment. If payment occurs, it is additional (e.g., in the form of a sign-up premium) and very low. Early examples of conscription (other than that of Peter the Great, which, as we have seen, can be termed 'indirect') can be found, for instance in the *conscription navale* introduced by Jean-Baptiste Colbert in the French navy to replace the earlier press-gangs and in Hesse and Hannover, but the breakthrough of conscription came in the French Revolution.

The army of the French Republic was at first a motley collection of remnants of the royal army of the Bourbons, militias and volunteers, but this clearly could not fulfil the military requirements of revolutionary France when it was attacked on all sides. The famous convention decree of August 1793 introduced throughout France the individual obligation (and right) of every French citizen to be a soldier. In doing so, it of course brought with it a need to define clearly who was a French citizen and who was not. At least in theory, the point of departure was the *armement général du peuple*. In practice, however, this first *levée en masse* of 1793, through which an army of 400,000 was raised, did not really constitute the start of conscription. The obligation to serve was a general one, but by and large those who served were volunteers. Real conscription was introduced five years later – when revolutionary fervour had worn off and the number of volunteers had dwindled – under the *Loi Jourdan* of September 1798. The system was exploited to the limits of its possibilities – and beyond – by Napoleon Bonaparte.[25]

After the restoration, France, like most other countries, largely abandoned universal conscription in exchange for a standing army of professionals, reinforced with long-term conscripts from the poorest sections of the population (precisely at the time when the French officers who figure in Fahmy's chapter introduced conscription in the Egyptian army). In France, the middle class was in practice almost completely exempt under a system which allowed those who were drafted to send, or pay for, a replacement. This, in fact, is a universal feature of early conscription systems in countries as far apart as France and Russia, and it confronted the state and its ruling elite with the dilemma that for its survival it depended on an army recruited from among those who had the least stake in society and might be politically least reliable (in addition to being the worst educated). This problem became more acute with the rise of socialism in the later nineteenth century. As Zürcher's chapter shows, in the Ottoman Empire exemptions were a particularly intractable problem, because, at least until 1909, Christians and Jews were not expected to serve and the burden fell on the Muslim population alone.

Conscription systems, such as the French, which relied on relatively long periods of service (eight years and over), resulted in relatively large and expensive standing armies, which, however, could not be strengthened in wartime by calling up a trained reserve. It also kept a large number of males away from the labour market during their most productive years. This problem was solved in Prussia by the army reforms which were introduced gradually after the defeat at Jena in 1806 and which resulted in the Law on Conscription of September 1814. Under this law, the male population was required to serve between one and three years in the regular frontline army, followed by service in the first- and second-class reserve (*Landwehr*) and finally in the *Landsturm* militia, which was activated only in the event of an enemy invasion. This hugely influential model combined the advantages of a relatively small standing army manned largely by professionals and volunteers with the availability of a large pool of trained reserves who could be called up in time of war. For the proper working of the system the linkages between the regular army and the reserve were essential. This later led to the dissolution of the separate structure of the reserve, with reservists filling out regular units rather than serving in their own, a practice followed by the Ottomans on the eve of World War I.[26]

The Prussian system proved its effectiveness in the wars of 1866 and 1870, and as a result all European countries except the United Kingdom adopted 'universal' compulsory military service as a defensive measure even in peacetime. In the Ottoman Empire the conscription system introduced in 1844 was modelled largely on the Prussian example, and after 1870 Prussian/German influence grew markedly; eventually, the system became well-nigh universal. Even those countries where there was great reluctance to employ it, like the United States and Britain, succumbed. The US used the system temporarily during the Civil War and in the great wars of the twentieth century, finally abandoning the draft towards the end of the Vietnam war in 1969. Britain adopted conscription when General Kitchener's army ran short of volunteers in 1916 and even reintroduced 'national service' after World War II, only reverting to a professional army in 1963. It is only since the end of the Cold War around 1990 that conscription seems to be on the wane in most of the industrialized world.

Military considerations apart, conscript armies have been seen as prime instruments for nation-building. This was already recognised in the nineteenth century, but it became especially important in the new nation-states created during the break-up of empires after World War I and during the decolonization process after World War II. Cronin points out the importance of this factor in the Middle East.

There are a number of prerequisites for the successful introduction of a conscript army. First of all, a reliable census has to be in place to determine where the potential manpower can be found. This requires a sizeable growth in the state bureaucracy quite apart from the purely military apparatus. Then, an efficient apparatus for the actual recruitment and, in almost every case, efficient sanctions (such as '*cantonnement*' of troops in the houses of those who refuse to turn up, or hostage-taking of family members) to combat desertion have to be put in place.[27] In most cases service was determined by the drawing of lots, in which case a system of lottery has to be introduced and executed. The troops have to be moved, fed, clothed and armed in much larger numbers than before, which presupposes a certain degree of economic efficiency, or even industrialization, which was non-existent in the Ottoman Empire or Persia. Raw recruits from the countryside have to be educated and trained so as not to lower the efficiency of the standing professional army too much – quantity should not endanger quality. Some of the fiercest resistance to general conscription has in fact come from within the professional army for this very reason.

The use of an army of conscripts also had far-reaching consequences for the way war was waged and the way it was presented to the population. As war now involved the whole population, mobilizing and motivating that population through the use of propaganda acquired an altogether novel importance (evolving into the concept of the 'Home Front' in World War I). Likewise, breaking the enemy's will (and that is, after all, according to Clausewitz the ultimate goal of any warfare) now also involved breaking the will to resist of the enemy population, not only of the army in the field. The concept of a 'nation in arms' almost inevitably led to different behaviour of the army vis-à-vis the enemy population, as was demonstrated during the Franco-Prussian war of 1870. Guerrilla warfare had its origins in the aftermath of the French Revolution (when the Spanish first used the term for their popular resistance against Napoleon's occupying forces), and the use of '*franc-tireurs*' by the French in the 1870 war was in this tradition. It blurred the distinction between soldiers and civilians even further and led to hostage-taking and random shootings by the Germans which presaged the tragedies of Oradour and My Lai in the twentieth century.

The reliability of the conscript armies was always a worry in the minds of the General Staff, though in the event even the enormous hordes of conscripts thrown into battle in World War I proved remarkably resilient. Only after three years of almost incredibly ferocious fighting did the first major signs of dissent appear (the famous mutiny of May 1917 in the French army), but even then it was fairly easily put down. But in a sense the generals were right, of course: the conscripts were essentially civilians in uniform and by sheer weight of numbers they tended to determine the atmosphere in the armies more and more. In the long run this necessitated a different style of leadership, at least in those countries where the population became more literate, wealthy and mobile. The American armies in both world wars and today's NATO forces are examples of this trend. In exchange for the willingness of the populations to fight and to keep on fighting, hardpressed governments had to make promises of social justice ('A land fit for heroes to live in'). In the aftermath both of World War I and of World War II these promises were at least partly fulfilled, leading to the welfare state after 1945.

The options of the recruit: A repertoire of resistance

Turning from the state and its concerns to the those at the receiving end of its policies, we should now try to catalogue the possible reactions to military recruitment, to see which types of resistance may be expected in which situations.

The most outspoken resistance may be expected where new forms of recruitment are introduced, where the rules are changed dramatically (as in the case of the introduction of conscription) or when circumstances change dramatically (for example, when war breaks out or when wars are lost).

The decision whether to resist at all and the choice of a particular form of resistance depend essentially on two things: the assessment of the balance between advantages and disadvantages of military service, and the available resources and repertoires of action. Neither factor can be analysed simply as a result of individual calculations on the part of the recruit. As his immediate relatives are severely affected as well, the resistance should really be analysed in the framework of household strategies. The way resistance will express itself is heavily dependent on the repertoire of action that is available, both within the community of origin and in the army.

The balance between advantages and disadvantages

What may be an advantage to one young man in his prime may be a disadvantage to another. Where the prospective mercenary, his relatives and his future bride will see the army as a (rare) job opportunity or a possibility to enhance their status, most conscripts and their families will blame the army for loss of income or worse. The disadvantage will be all the greater if service in the army involves immediate risks such as undernourishment, disease, mistreatment (spectacular in the case of Mehmed Ali's army, as described by Fahmy) or danger. Obviously all these aggravating circumstances count more in times of war than in peacetime. The longer the service, the worse the recruit's prospects of ever returning to his village. It is said that, in Russian villages, the departure of the recruits was sometimes 'celebrated' with a funeral ceremony. In the Ottoman Empire, a whole body of military songs exists which depicts conscription as a death sentence.[28]

Resources and repertoires of action

The available resources of avoidance and resistance are clearly linked to the way in which recruitment is organized. If we restrict ourselves to conscription only, we have to take into consideration the degree to which the state was able to muster the bureaucratic force to execute the system effectively. As noted earlier, this involved registration, medical examinations, regulations about exemptions, the drawing of lots, the actual enrolment, transport and drilling. Obviously, making use of each of these stages in the process to avoid recruitment was far easier in a state, like the Ottoman in the nineteenth century and the Persian in the early twentieth, where the bureaucracy was still being created than in one of the established bureaucratic states of Europe.

Opportunities are not the only determining factor, however. The forms of resistance are 'path-dependent': they depend on the existing traditions of avoidance and resistance in the army and navy and in society at large.

Resistance can take many forms. The recruit can try to avoid recruitment by going into hiding. In Anatolia and the Balkans, 'leaving for the mountains' to escape the demands of the state was an age-old tradition. From the seventeenth century onwards, the lowland tracts close to the main roads had become a wasteland and communities had withdrawn into the mountains. Brigandage was very widespread even in the early twentieth century. Another strategy, available to those with enough means, was leaving the country temporarily or for good (or taking a different nationality, as many Ottoman Greeks and Armenians did after 1909); an Ottoman Muslim recruit could convert to Christianity or – the opposite solution – perform the *Hajj*, the Muslim pilgrimage: the chapters by Zürcher and Douwes give us examples of both. He could mutilate himself in order to be sent home (a strategy employed in all armies, but apparently very widespread in Mehmed Ali's Egyptian army).

Of course, the soldier can try to desert, either on the way to the front or through the enemy lines.[29] The first seems to have been very widespread in the Ottoman army, both because of its lax controls and because it was socially acceptable to the villagers. The second was rare, at least if the enemy was Christian.

Soldiers contemplating resistance of any kind of course have to take into account the risks and the penalty that may have to be paid. These penalties were always more severe than in civilian life because soldiers are dealt with under martial, that is to say criminal, law.[30]

Strategies like avoidance or desertion seem individual but they do require the support of household, family or village. If desertion is not an option, the recruit can strike or refuse to carry out orders, and, finally, he can rebel and mutiny. All these are collective actions which require organization. As the risks of overt resistance are great, these ultimate means will be avoided as long as possible. If practiced these will tend to take the form of peaceful demonstrations and petitions, rather than open revolt. Families, too, may play a part. As they are not under the constraints of military discipline, they can often protest more easily than the men themselves. In the case of a Dutch naval mutiny in 1779, the seamen's wives sent an anonymous letter to the Admiralty board reminding its members that their wearing of expensive wigs was made possible only because they – the wives – had nothing but cabbage stalks to eat ('want voor ons geld soo draegen de heeren pruijke en wij moeten eete koolstruijke').[31] If an open revolt comes to pass, the participants will act as one unit, avoiding individual liability. A clear example from naval mutinies is the device known as a 'Round Robin'. This is a written declaration; it was described in 1716 as follows:

> They take a large Sheet of Paper, and strike two Circles, one a good distance without the other; in the inner Circle, they will write what they have a mind to have done; and between the two Circular Lines, they write their Names, in and out, against the Circles; beginning like the four Cardinal points of the Compass, right opposite to each other, and so continue till the Paper is filled; which appears in a Circle, and no one can be said to be first, so that they all are equally guilty: Which I believe to be contrived to keep 'em all firm to their purpose, when once they have signed it; and if discovered, no one can be excused, by saying, he was the last that signed it, and he had not done it without great Persuasion.[32]

Different armies have had to face different forms of resistance. In France, for example, the General Staff was convinced that the entire army was 'rotten' when desertions increased from around 500 in 1914 to 21,000 in 1917,[33] but the much smaller Ottoman army by 1918 had half a million deserters. On the other hand, mutinies were almost unheard-of in the Ottoman army of World War I, even when the soldiers were barefoot and starving.[34] Clearly, here the 'path', the pre-existing strategy of which the soldiers could avail themselves, was missing. Mutinies had been a common phenomenon in the pre-modern Ottoman army. Many *coups d'état* had started with the Janissaries turning over their soup kettles. But the conscript armies of Egypt and the Ottoman Empire were armies of peasants who came from a very different tradition from that of the town- and city-based Janissaries with their strong esprit de corps. Strikes were not unknown in the empire – closing down the bazaar was a traditional means of protest, and industrial strikes proliferated after 1908 – but they were limited to the few centres (Salonica, Istanbul, Izmir, Bursa) where a small industrial workforce had come into being in the late nineteenth century.[35] Again, both traditions were alien to the village population which made up the bulk of the army.

Because of the enormous difficulties and penalties involved in all forms of resistance, here, too, we have to abstain from a one-sided analysis of recruits as individuals, detached from their communities of origin. As many contributions to this volume make clear, these communities are important, not only in weighing advantages against disadvantages (although, admittedly, in the case of conscription the disadvantages far outweighed any advantages), but also in the acts of avoidance and resistance. Emigration, flight, hiding, self-mutilation, bribery – none of these can be practiced without the help of one's relatives. Because the actual or future household is at stake, all these acts can be interpreted as household strategies.

Anxiety about the survival of the families they left behind was also often a morale-sapping issue for the conscripts. The detailed provisions made by the Ottoman government for 'families left without breadwinner' (*muinsiz aile*), described in Chapter 7 by Nicole van Os, show the official concerns on this point. At least this was a more benign sort of attention than that displayed by the Russian government, which in the 1830s launched a propaganda campaign praising mothers who turned in their fugitive sons and awarding informers a special silver medal inscribed 'for diligence'.[36]

The structure of this collection involves a journey through time and space. Virginia Aksan and Daniel Panzac start us off by drawing a picture of the traditional recruitment systems in the land forces and the navy of the Ottoman Empire on the eve of the introduction of conscription. Then Khaled Fahmy presents the story of the army of Mehmed Ali Pasha of Egypt, who pioneered conscription in the Middle East, and Erik Jan Zürcher describes how the Ottoman Empire organized its recruiting system when it answered the pasha's challenge. Nicole van Os shows us that the state realized that it had to take care not only of its soldiers, but also of their families. Where Zürcher and van Os deal primarily with decision-making at the centre, Dick Douwes and Odile Moreau show us the impact new recruiting methods had in Ottoman provinces as far apart as Syria and Bosnia. Sergei Kudryashov and, lastly, Stephanie Cronin, take us to areas further east, where conscription became an issue only in the early twentieth century, causing widespread resistance in Central Asia and Iran.

It is hoped that these studies combined will allow the reader to see that both where conscription as part of the formation of modern states is concerned, and where the focus is on the repertoire of resistance of individuals, households and communities, there are striking similarities not only between the different countries of the Middle East but also between the Middle East and Europe. The logic of state formation and the reactions it encounters clearly transcends boundaries of civilisations.

Notes

1   There is a sizeable literature on conscription by *military* historians. It is, however, devoted almost exclusively to North America and Europe. Martin Anderson, *Conscription: A Select and Annotated Bibliography* (Stanford, 1976), has 413 pages of entries, of which twenty are devoted to countries other than the US and the UK. The countries dealt with under 'other foreign countries' are exclusively European or British Empire dominions. The authors are indebted to Lex Heerma van Voss for his helpful comments and additional information.

2   An inspiring example is Stephen Peter Rosen, *Societies and Military Power: India and its Armies* (Delhi, 1996) with his daring comparisons. See, for example, p. 28: 'Rather than arguing that Christian, Islamic, Hispanic or Hindu cultures each have specific, constant, and unique strategic outlooks, we can look at each political unit in each culture area and ask what the dominant structures are, what effects they have for the ability to generate military power, what relation the military has to society, and whether those structures and relations are changing.'

3   Charles Tilly, *Coercion, Capital and European States, 990–1900* (Cambridge, MA, 1990).

4   Because of the analytical point of view chosen, the relation between the feudal lord and his soldiers will not be discussed here; however, it will be clear that – as in the case of the relation between the state and its subjects, to be discussed below – here we also have all sorts of variations between free and unfree relations. A good example is the Hessian subsidy troops employed by, among others, the Dutch and later especially the English (e.g., in the American War of Liberation) which can be seen as capitalist hiring of mercenaries. However, within Hessen both feudal obligations and, in the second half of the eighteenth century, conscription also play an important role. See Peter K. Taylor, *Indentured to Liberty: Peasant Life and the Hessian Military State 1688–1815* (Ithaca, NY, and London, 1994).

5 For a sophisticated discussion of state–peasant relations in the Ottoman
   Empire, see Huri İslamoğlu-İnan, *State and Peasant in the Ottoman Empire:
   Agrarian Power Relations and Regional Economic Development in Ottoman
   Anatolia during the Sixteenth Century* (Leiden, 1994), pp. 1–21. The
   bibliography gives an excellent introduction to the debate on feudalism.

6 For the transition, see Suraiya Faroqhi, 'Crisis and Change', in Halil
   İnalcık with Donald Quataert, eds., *An Economic and Social History of the
   Ottoman Empire 1300–1914* (Cambridge, 1994), pp. 413–622.

7 We must bear in mind that only after the Crimean War did the Ottomans
   cease to enslave prisoners of war or enemy subjects (Y.H. Erdem, *Slavery
   in the Ottoman Empire and its Demise, 1800–1909* (Basingstoke and London,
   1996). However, in the nineteenth century these slaves were no longer
   recruited for the army or navy.

8 Henry H. Hirschbiel, 'Conscription in Russia', in Joseph L. Wiecynski,
   ed., *The Modern Encyclopedia of Russian and Soviet History* (55 vols., 1978),
   vol. 8, pp. 4–9; P. Kolchin, *Unfree Labor: American Slavery and Russian
   Serfdom* (Cambridge, MA, 1987), pp. 42, 204, 367–8.

9 Christopher Lloyd, *The British Seaman, 1200–1860: A Social Survey*
   (London, 1968). See also Daniel Panzac's chapter in this volume.

10 Daniel Pipes, *Slave Soldiers and Islam: The Genesis of a Military System*
   (New Haven and London, 1981), p. 100.

11 Pipes, *Slave Soldiers and Islam*; Stephen Peter Rosen, *Societies and Military
   Power. India and its Armies* (Delhi, 1996), pp. 114–15, 119–23; İsmail
   Hakkı Uzunçarşılı, *Kapıkulu Ocakları* (2 vols, Ankara, 1943–4).

12 This is why the Ottomans rejected the possibility of recruiting the children
   of townspeople.

13 See André Zysberg, *Les Galériens: Vies et destins de 6000 forcats sur les
   galères de France 1680–1748* (Paris, 1987); Frederick C. Lane, *Venice: A
   Maritime Republic* (Baltimore, 1973), pp. 364–79, 414–15.

14 In the eighteenth century galleys vanished from the Mediterranean but
   became popular in the Baltic. There the Russians deployed serfs under
   their new conscription system, but other nations used free oarsmen.

15 Jan Lucassen, 'The International Maritime Labour Market (C16th–19th)',
   in P. van Royen, J.R. Bruijn and J. Lucassen, eds., *'Those emblems of hell'?
   European sailors and maritime labour market, 1570–1870* [Research in
   Maritime History 13] (St. John's, NF, 1997), pp. 11–23; K. van der
   Tempel, '"Wij hebben amok in ons schip": Aziaten in opstand tijdens drie
   terugreizen op het einde van de achttiende eeuw', in J.R. Bruijn and E.S.
   van Eyck van Heslinga, eds., *Muiterij: Oproer en berechting op schepen van
   de VOC* (Haarlem, 1980), pp. 123–47.

16 Gregory Hanlon, 'The Decline of a Provincial Military Aristocracy: Siena
   1560–1740', *Past and Present* 155 (May 1997), pp. 64–108.

17 For Hessians, see Taylor, *Indentured to Liberty*. For Scots, see T.C.

Smout, N.C. Landsman and T.M. Devine, 'Scottish Emigration in the Seventeenth and Eighteenth Centuries', in Nicholas Canny, ed., *Europeans on the Move: Studies on European Migration, 1500–1800* (Oxford, 1994), pp. 76–112; Thomas C. Smout, 'Scots and Emigrants in Europe, 1400–1700', in Simonetta Cavaciocchi, ed., *Le migrazioni in Europa secc. XIII–XVIII* (Prato, 1994), pp. 659–69; and Dmitry G. Fedosov, 'Russia's Scottish Clans', in Cavaciocchi, *Le migrazioni in Europa*, pp. 861–6. For Irish, see Robert A. Stradling, 'Military Recruitment and Movement as a Form of Migration: Spain and its Irish Mercenaries, 1598–1665', in Cavaciocchi, *Le migrazioni in Europa*, pp. 477–90; and L.M. Cullen, 'The Irish Diaspora of the Seventeenth and Eighteenth Centuries', in Canny, *Europeans on the Move*, pp. 113–49.

18 Janice E. Thomson, *Mercenaries, Pirates and Sovereigns: State-building and Extraterritorial Violence in Early Modern Europe* (Princeton, 1994).

19 Geoffery Fisher, *Barbary Legend: War, Trade and Piracy in North Africa, 1415–1830* (Oxford, 1957).

20 Catherine Wendy Bracewell, *The Uskoks of Senj: Piracy, Banditry and the Holy War in the Sixteenth-Century Adriatic* (Ithaca, NY, and London, 1992).

21 Suraiya Faroqhi, *Pilgrims and Sultans: The Hajj under the Ottomans 1517–1683* (London, 1994), pp. 54–73.

22 Sweden drafted soldiers in the countryside with the help of farmers' communities from the 17th century onwards. Brian M. Downing, *The Military Revolution and political change. Origins of democracy and autocracy in early modern Europe* (Princeton, 1992) 187–211; Jan Lindegren, "The Swedish 'Military State', 1560–1720", in: *Scandinavian Journal of History* 10 (1985) 305–336.]

23 Lane, *Venice*.

24 See Taylor, *Indentured to Liberty*.

25 See Alan Forrest, *Conscripts and Deserters: The Army and French Society during the Revolution and Empire* (Oxford, 1989).

26 Heinz Stübig, Die Wehrverfassung Preußen in der Reformzeit. Wehrpflicht im Spannungsfeld von Restauration und Revolution, 1815–1860 in: Roland G. Foerster, ed, *Die Wehrpflicht Entstehen, Erscheinungsformen und politisch-militärische Wirkung* (München, 1994), pp 39–55.

27 See, for examples in the Netherlands, Alex Barten and Frans Kraan, '*Stelligen Onwil': Dienstweigering tijdens de Belgische Opstand* (Amsterdam, 1996).

28 Erik Jan Zürcher, 'Little Mehmet in the Desert. The Ottoman Soldier's Experience', in Hugh Cecil and Peter Liddle, eds., *Facing Armageddon: The First World War Experienced* (London, 1996), pp. 230–41.

29 Ulrich Broeckling and Michael Sikora (eds.), *Armeen und ihre Deserteure,*

Vernachlässigte Kapittel einer Militärgeschichte der Neuzeit (Göttingen 1998).

30 Outside the Anglo-Saxon world, where breach of contract still fell under criminal law until very late (in Britain until 1875–1877), in most European countries labour contracts (except for sailors) fell under civil law. This is important distinction between military and civilian jobs. Cf. R.J. Steinfeld, *The Invention of Free Labor. The Employment Relation in English and American Law and Culture, 1350–1870)* (Chapell Hill and London, 1991) and for late examples of unfree labour in the Dutch merchant marine; Peter B. Schuman, *Tussen vlag en voorschip: een eeuw wettelijke en maatschappelijke emancipatie van zeevarenden ter Nederlandse koopvaardij, 1838–1940* (Amsterdam 1995).

31 Jaap R. Bruijn, *The Dutch Navy of the Seventeenth and Eighteenth Centuries* (Columbia, SC, 1993), p. 206.

32 Marcus Rediker, *Between the Devil and the Deep Blue Sea: Merchant Seamen, Pirates, and the Anglo-American Maritime World, 1700–1750* (Cambridge, 1987), p. 234; D.L.M. Weijers, '"Dappere waterleeuwen versus schelmen": een muiterij in Perzische wateren, 1733', in J.R. Bruijn and E.S. van Eyck van Heslinga, eds., *Muiterij: Oproer en berechting op schepen van de VOC* (Haarlem, 1980), pp. 44–57.

33 Leonard Smith, 'The French High Command and the Mutinies of Spring 1917', in Hugh Cecil and Peter Liddle, eds., *Facing Armageddon: The First World War Experienced* (London, 1996), pp. 79–92.

34 Erik Jan Zürcher, 'Between Death and Desertion: The Experience of the Ottoman Soldier in World War I', *Turcica* 28 (1996), pp. 235–58.

35 See Donald Quataert, *Social Disintegration and Popular Resistance in the Ottoman Empire, 1881–1908* (New York, 1983).

36 Kolchin, *Unfree Labor*, pp. 284–283.

1· Ottoman Military Recruitment Strategies in the Late Eighteenth Century

Virginia H. Aksan

The Ottoman Empire is generally characterized as one of the most militarized societies of early modern Europe. The iconography of the Janissaries, whose gunpowder weapons, zeal, discipline and ferocity astonished observers in the sixteenth and seventeenth centuries, commands an audience even today. Lurid tales of their decline into an unruly rabble by the eighteenth century, which dominate the general surveys of Ottoman history, have prevented a more complex view of the evolution of the Ottoman military from emerging.[1] While it is generally conceded that by the middle of the eighteenth century the Janissaries were unequal to the task of defending the empire, a discussion of their replacements in this transition period is only now beginning. This chapter offers a framework to redress the neglect, by suggesting that the nineteenth-century Ottoman army evolved from a combination of voluntary feudatory militias and Janissary-style conscripted infantries into a system of state-funded militias, with periods of short-term conscription, particularly in the 1768–74 Russo-Turkish War. Though the transition to a system of theoretically universal conscription was not completed until the era of the 'Trained Victorious Muhammadan Soldiers' of Mahmud II (1808–39), it will be argued that after 1750 the Ottomans accelerated mobilization practices which anticipated the 'New Model Army' (*Nizam-i Cedid*) of Selim III (1789–1807), and, in fact, influenced its composition and sources of manpower.

Discussion of that evolution is dependent on a number of assumptions, the first one being that Ottoman military strategy was driven as a response to both endemic internal and external violence, much as European dynasties struggled to balance the two by creating standing armies out of the landless and unemployed, a view which has linked militarization and the articulation of the modern state.[2] This seems particularly apt in the Ottoman context, where control of internal violence and defence of shrinking borders drove mobilization and military fiscalism in the late eighteenth century, and propelled the emergence of Ottoman mid-nineteenth-century absolutism. That is to say that the escalation of war required more army, hence, more taxes and more bureaucracy. Successive wars increased indebtedness, which required further intrusion into the countryside in order to finance mobilization and supply, through a process of oppression and negotiation with native elites which gradually reduced the political autonomy of local communities. Changing Ottoman strategies for manning the battlefield both reflect similar developments in European armies, and also represent a continuation of earlier Ottoman practice.

Secondly, the cultural adaptation required to make the transition to European-style discipline and hierarchies of command, far more disruptive in the end of Ottoman household dynamics and political legitimacy, is less immediately apparent in this transitional period. What is apparent is the (re)construction of a Muslim army, ultimately both exclusionary and punitive. The manpower for these late Ottoman armies was drawn exclusively from Muslim, often nomadic or tribal, sources, part of a deliberate policy but also influenced by the increasingly restricted territory as the borders shrank. The secularization and rationalization of making war forced a conscription strategy which professed universality but in reality was restricted largely to Muslim peasants, and which replaced volunteerism with coercion, denying pious loyalties but maintaining Muslim iconography in service to state-driven priorities.

Maintaining massive armies, often larger than the population of many of the towns and cities of the continent, was a pattern of development which occured in European societies of the eighteenth century as well. The logistics of making war were a considerable problem, as is suggested by estimates about late-seventeenth-century warfare: an army of 60,000 soldiers required a daily ration of 45 tons of bread, 40,000 gallons of beer, 200–300 hundred head of cattle for meat, and 90 tons of fodder for animals.[3] According to one source, a wagon train 198 kilometres long was required to feed an army of similar size for a month.[4] Military strategists of the eighteenth century estimated that 100 wagons a day were required to supply 50,000 men who were 15 miles, or one to two days' march, from their base.[5] Pre-modern societies found their capacity to sustain warfare stretched to its natural limit, forcing a rethinking and gradual rationalization of both men and supplies.

Armies made up of multi-ethnic federative forces were gradually superseded by more cohesive, but costly, standing armies made up of native volunteers and recruits, the flotsam and jetsam of rural society, and, latterly, conscripts. Local feudatory lords, who mobilized and supplied their own troops, were replaced by the military contractors and suppliers of competing states, the most obvious example being the France of the Bourbons, which moved from an army of 'aggregrate contract[s]' to 'state commission[s]' to 'popular conscription' by 1800 in order to mobilize and supply the most massive army of Europe.[6]

In similar fashion, the Ottomans evolved an eighteenth-century standing army by increasing use of the armed irregular, the *levend*. Many of the same imperatives of the European versions operated in the Ottoman context, even if the means were different. The *levend* regiments recruited for the Russo-Ottoman wars which began in 1768 represented an army parallel to the Janissaries, often numerically greater, and replacing the completely useless benefice-style soldiers (the *timariot*s or *sipahi*s).[7]

By the late fourteenth century, the Ottomans had created a standing army, the converted slave army of the Janissaries, an elite, highly educated infantry corps, drawn from tributary Christian children (the *devşirme* system), primarily from the European territories of the new empire. Ottoman logistical mastery was well ahead of similar developments in European military thinking, and was based on a system of well-maintained roads and warehouses, to allow for the smooth passage of the army to battlefronts both west and east. This was the organization which startled the Austrian envoy de Busbecq, eye-witness to the camp of Süleyman the Magnificent, into warning his Austrian masters of their potential threat.[8]

The system had been allowed to fall into disarray after the 1660s, and the Janissaries had become 'an almost unpaid militia, made up of small tradesmen whose main rewards were judicial and tax immunities, which they were increasingly unable to justify on the battlefield'.[9] Increasingly such a force was ineffective in the kinds of warfare in which the Ottomans were engaged, partly because of a typical, elite military resistance to innovation, but more particularly because of their gradual merging with rural and urban society, what one might characterize as the gentrification of the military. Preservation of the privilege of being a Janissary remained the primary aim of the new gentry, however, and is reflected in the long struggle against attempts to reform the army muster rolls, and the revolts thus engendered, one of the most damaging being the 1730 revolt in Istanbul.[10]

The single greatest privilege of the corps, registration in such rolls, and a soldier's certificate (*esame*), guaranteed both the monthly salary and the daily rations, or their monetary equivalent. The entire Ottoman bureaucracy, up to and including the grand vizier, profited from the salaries of fictional lists of combatants. Corrupted rolls remained the most intractable problem in the Janissary organization, similar to that facing all the armies of Europe of the period, as thousands of mini-armies or militias, commanded by officers who ran their own troops as corporations, were gradually drawn under state control.

Ottoman eighteenth-century battle strength was based on such rolls. By the end of the century, of a possible 400,000 such chits in circulation, only 10 per cent may have represented live soldiers ready for duty.[11] Janissary pay and ration tickets had begun to be sold and traded in the market in the reign of Mahmud I (1730–54), a system which, as noted, benefited Ottoman administrators at large. A particularly interesting example is Grand Vizier Çelebi Mehmed Pasha, whose brief career in 1778 ended with the discovery in his possession of pay tickets representing 12,700 akçe (asper) a day.[12] The average soldier in the Janissary system probably never received more than a maximum of 20 akçe a day in this period, suggesting that the grand vizier possessed *esame*s representing over 600 soldiers![13] Such a profitable trade, which meant that thousands of non-combatants were enriched, while many an ordinary soldier went unpaid, was especially difficult to reform. The majority of the advisors to Sultan Selim III cited the *esame* as the chief problem surrounding the Janissary corps, and almost universally recommended the reform of the rolls.

The breakdown of the Janissaries' fighting capability meant that the Ottomans had to accelerate alternative systems to face the greatest challenge to their power in the Russia of Catherine the Great, which, by 1750, was maintaining the world's largest standing army on one-fifth of the revenues of the French monarchy.[14] The 1699 reforms of Peter the Great created a new standing army, but the countryside had become used to mobilization a half century earlier. In the 1680s, the Russian standing army was more than 200,000 strong, representing 4.4 per cent of the population.[15] During Peter's reign, there were fifty-three levies for a total of more than 300,000 recruits.[16] For the 1768–74 war alone, under Catherine II, 300,000 troops were levied.[17] By 1795, the standing army numbered 450,000.[18] Russia relied on the conscription of serfs, for whom mobilization meant a lifetime sentence (for twenty-five years only after 1793). Self-mutilation was a frequent method of avoiding the levy.[19] Certainly one of the causes of the massive Pugachev rebellion of 1773, started among the Cossacks, and led by a Cossack officer, was the strain that conscription and constant warfare in the south had begun to put on the populace at large. Other causes of revolt during the Russo-Turkish wars, such as the devastation of agriculture and the destruction of human and animal life, are fairly well documented for the Russian side, less so for the Ottomans. Death by cholera and plague as well as combat were endemic (to Russian and Ottoman armies alike), with losses as high as 25 per cent, and sometimes closer to 50 per cent on the long forced marches, when desertion made armies vanish into thin air.[20] Distance and food supply were a continual preoccupation in the Danubian context. Disease was particularly virulent in the region, and often accounted for more deaths than actual battlefield confrontations.

Still, the Russians had vast manpower resources on which to draw, and by 1800 had become master strategists against their primary foe on the Black Sea. Incorporation and settlement of new territories, and the curbing of Cossack and Tatar alike by the creation of separate regimental structures within the Russian army were part of the keys to their success. The Ottomans, by contrast, had a shrinking manpower supply, exacerbated by the assumed and demonstrably increasing unreliability of Christian populations in the border regions, particularly the client principalities of Wallachia and Moldavia, but also in Greece. For the Ottomans to reach a battlefront strength of 100,000 to 200,000, various recruitment strategies were used: the Janissaries, or standing army, local fortress and other provincial troops and levies of state-funded recruits (called *miri levendat*, or *miri askerî*) could all be mobilized for protecting the frontiers of the empire. As the Janissaries were effectively a fictional army, the remaining effective corps had to be supplemented by the latter groups, especially the levies, which had become the only way to get troops in any number to the battlefront. Just how fictional can be demonstrated by a roll call on the battlefront in late 1772, when more than 30,000 names were struck from the Janissary registers.[21]

The need for soldiers was especially great in 1768, when the Ottomans declared war on Russia. The army had to be rebuilt after a hiatus from fighting of some thirty years during which the Danube region had been relatively tranquil. The striking aspect of this period is the continued volunteerism and emphasis on individual valour evident in the campaigns that unfolded. One of the more confusing aspects is that official documentation appears to maintain a distinction between a Janissary and other types of soldiers, but on the ground, as eyewitness accounts indicate, everyone appears to be a Janissary or Janissary aspirant. The corps' iconography and privileges still drew volunteers, even though methods and sources of recruitment had changed. While the Janissaries are still recorded as a prominent part of the campaigns of 1768–74, at least nominally, the true cannon fodder was drawn from the Balkan and Anatolian peasantry, as well as from the landless and lawless. They were untrained, raw recruits. Anecdotal evidence suggests an acceleration of '*bedeliyat*', or substitutions, an attempt to avoid service by buying out: 25 to 30 *kuruş* per soldier seems to have done the trick,[22] but there is very little evidence of massive resistance to recruitment, probably because the control over populations thus raised was far less coercive than in the Russian context.

Raising troops locally as a strategy to augment or counterbalance the Janissaries was the continuation of an old practice in the constellation of the Ottoman forces. The Janissary corps, primarily infantry troops loyal to the sultan, was initially created to counteract the power of local feudatory forces, whose cavalry troops were given land grants (*timar*s) as salaries. The influence of the corps itself was subsequently checked by the recruitment of local irregular bands. These were called by any number of names: *levend, sarıca* and *sekban*, and began to appear as early as the sixteenth century.[23] *Sarıca* and *sekban* were armed infantry musketeers, similar to the local militias of Europe of the same period. Such troops were drawn from among the *levend*, a term which retains the meaning of 'hero' or 'adventurer', but which then conjured up the lawless. All of these terms also stood for 'independent soldiery companies', whose mobilization and demobilization have been linked to great rural upheavals such as the rebellions of the late sixteenth century.[24]

Roving bands, once organized into fighting forces, were called household *levend*, or state *levend*, the distinction being whether they were part of the provincial governors' personal forces (*kapılı* or *kapı halkı*) or were paid directly by the state (*miri*).[25] The bands were organized into companies (*bayrak* or *bölük*), generally of 50 soldiers, and could be either cavalry (*suvari*) or infantry (*piyade*). Their commander was a *bölükbaşı*.[26]

After 1700, the organization and control of such *levend* companies changed, tied to the growth of the provincial dynasties of local notables, the *ayan*s, who emerge as their leaders especially after the 1720s. The provincial *ayan*s represented a powerful source of manpower; their opportunity for aggrandizement and accumulation of wealth should be self-evident. Mobilization for the 1768–74 war was predicated on the ability to persuade these local magnates and the centrally appointed provincial judges, or *kadıs*,[27] to participate in the coercion and extraction required to get men and supplies to the battlefront. These militias were often used to curb the abuses of the centrally appointed military administrative class in the countryside, and sometimes to control countryside violence. Just as often, the militias instigated local rebellion. Ottoman strategy was to eliminate the militia-turned-bandits by arming the countryside for its own protection, and then enlisting the resulting bands for the next campaign.[28]

The *levend* regiments under discussion evolved to replace the *timariots*, whose few remaining numbers, no longer of any use as a military force, clung to their rights because of the entitlement value of the *timar*.[29] Equally arguably, these troops served as an alternative to Janissary recruitment, as the *devşirme* tributary system of recruitment had been completely abandoned by 1700. State-funded militias served as the majority of the troops for Mustafa III (1757–74), who feared increasing the number of the traditional forces, following upon their excesses under Ahmed III (1703–30).[30] Payment for such troops came directly from the centre, with a significant sign-on bonus part of the incentive, and enlistment periods of six months, with frequent two-month renewals. A very careful formula of rations accompanied the records of troop mobilization, with cash equivalents ascribed. In sum, these were infantry and cavalry troops, commanded most often by local provincial officers, resembling to some degree the milita of earlier periods in Europe, organized out of a central treasury.[31]

Most of the mobilization statistics for the Ottoman wars are unreliable, but a few samples of the *levend* troops present prior to the 1768 war can be used as illustrative of an ongoing practice. For example, at Egri, Hungary, in 1596 an estimated 15,000–20,000 *levend* and *sekban* troops were present, serving in the lengthy campaign against the Habsburgs that ended in 1603.[32] Figures for the eighteenth century are scattered, but one from a mobilization register for 1738 records that 6000 *miri levendat* were recruited for the Iranian front.[33]

Figures for the total size of the assembled forces in the Danubian basin in 1768–74 vary from 80,000 to 600,000, depending upon the source of information.[34] The most interesting figure derives from a contemporary source who gave a total of 254,900 for Janissaries and *miri levendat*.[35] This appears to represent the expectations of the government at the beginning of the war: 45 commanders were each to bring 1000–2000 *levend* recruits to the front, an initial recruitment of 45,000–90,000, not including their own entourages, which were often quite large, or the officers of the recruits.[36] According to d'Ohsson, 97 regiments of 1000 *miri askeri* each participated in 1769.[37] Thus, approximately 100,000 *miri levendat* may have reached the Danubian battlefront in 1769, suggesting a mobilization of perhaps twice that number of men from the countryside of the Balkans and Anatolia, less so from the Arab provinces of the empire. Adding an estimated 30,000–60,000 Janissaries, a figure closer to 130,000–160,000 is suggested as a realistic estimate for Ottoman mobilization for the first year of the campaign. The Janissaries continued to be paid from local taxation, but the *miri levendat* salaries were drawn from the privy purse, one of the main reasons for the increased Ottoman indebtedness by the end of the war.[38]

The documents of recruitment demonstrate the ways in which these troops were perceived by the state. Most orders for the mobilization recognized the lawless and landless as the source of the manpower, noting that their misbehaviour had been the cause of much harm to the countryside, but indicating also that the lack of campaigns had cut them off gainful employment. The orders announced the forthcoming campaign with Russia, and stressed the pressing need for soldiers. A general amnesty was extended to the miscreants, and instructions concerning their recruitment followed. Explicit also is the role of the local provincial officials (*ayan*s and *mutasarrıf*s: governors of *sancak*s, sub-divisions of a province, and *kadı*s) in the organization of the *miri levendat* troops.[39]

Companies (*bayrak*) of fifty *levend*, usually expressed in terms of 500 or 1000 soldiers (ten or twenty companies), were to be mobilized by local officials. Formulaic orders from Istanbul always included the number of soldiers, and several other items: the mobilization or sign-up bonus (*bahşiş*), the monthly salary (*ulufe*), in six-month lump sums, as the general estimated length of the campaign season, a 10 per cent commission for the officers (*ondalık*), and a calculation of the daily rations, similarly defined for six months service. Two-month periods were also often specified, sometimes as an extension of service, sometimes for winter quarters, for passage to the front, or for fortress duty.

These were contractual troops, paid from the central treasury, and guaranteed by regional notables who could be fined double the advance from the imperial treasury for the desertion of their soldiers, although the fine was rarely imposed. Local officials were also responsible for the appointment of the company commander, often the *mutasarrıf* himself.

Many of them became commanders of various divisions of the battlefront, and were generally very important in sustaining the Ottoman campaigns throughout the war.[40] The ratio of cavalry to infantry varied from an estimated two to one (1770) to an estimated one in four (ca. 1810).[41]

The purpose of the sign-on bonus was probably to equip a *levend* with either with a gun or a horse.[42] It certainly also served as an enticement to impoverished young men, the attraction universal to military service. Many of the orders for *levend* call for expert marksmen, without explicitly stating that they must own a weapon. Small arms and their distribution were under the jurisdiction of the imperial armoury, while guns were generally destined for the various Janissary corps. According to one observer, even the Janissary was expected to supply his own arms, and at the battlefront weapons were distributed only to those who had none.[43] There is much evidence to suggest that the armoury possessed prodigious quantities of weapons, but little information on their distribution.[44] Fear of armed populations was no less an Ottoman than a European obsession. Similarly, hiring an armed soldier parallels the European situation in the eighteenth century, but the word 'armed' should be used with caution. One eye-witness of this war remarked that recruits who enlisted for the Ottoman side came armed with clubs as weapons, complaining that a sword or a rifle was too expensive.[45]

Daily rations in the *miri levendat* records were of four or five staples: bread and meat for both infantry and cavalry, but additionally rice, cooking fat, and barley were calculated for the horses of the cavalry. The *levend* infantryman at war was expected to need a daily intake of a double loaf of bread and more than a pound of meat (over 600 grams), the equivalent of the Janissary rations. The cavalryman was entitled to the same amount of bread, but half the amount of meat, (roughly 300 grams), plus a similar amount of rice, 80 grams of cooking oil or fat, and roughly 6.5 kilograms of barley per day per man for fodder. These rations were far more generous than those of the Russian soldier, who was expected to live on rye flour and groats to make gruel (*kasha*),[46] and forage for the rest. The Ottoman formulas may well have been unrealizable on the battlefront; perhaps Russian expectations were more realistic. Cash substitution for rations became the norm on the Ottoman side, certainly by the end of the war, calculated as part of the formula in the documents, and probably never equivalent to battlefield prices, inflated by scarcity and hoarding.

The state records throughout this period continue to make a clear distinction between the Janissary troops and the irregular *levend*, but at the provincial level the two appear often to have been conflated. *Levend* troops are everywhere, side by side with Janissaries, in the fortresses as well as in the large-scale battles, rare in this war. An attempt was made to eradicate the use of the term '*levend*' by the government in 1775 because of the evocation of the disasters of the recent war.[47] Still, the accounts for the *levend* troops continue in exactly the same manner in the register used in this study, but the word '*asakir*' (singular: *asker*, 'soldier') replaced '*levend*' in 1777.[48] The two had come to mean the same thing to Ottoman officials. The last date in the register is 1789.

The 1768–74 war was therefore crucial in the Ottoman evolution to a more 'modern' standing army, in the increased enrolment of infantry and cavalry regiments from indigenous, Muslim, landless populations, and their payment from central treasury funds. The combination of volunteer and conscripted men also indicates an army in transition from the original forced recruitment of the Janissaries in the fourteenth century, through federative militias to regiments of state-funded militias to the new conscript army of the nineteenth century.

The 1787–92 campaigns, however, broke the back of the traditional forces altogether. Statistics of recruitment and active forces for that war, much as with the previous one, are exaggerated and unreliable, and as yet remain unstudied to any degree. The problem of the elusive nature of information on the Ottomans' true military force of the period was acutely observed in the early 1800s:

Sir James Porter [British Ambassador to the Ottoman Empire] considers the army to be composed of the body of the people, and the janizaries to amount to two to three hundred thousand men, independently of those who get themselves enrolled to enjoy the privileges. Pey[s]sonnel supposes they may consist of many millions. Baron de Tott calculates them to be four hundred thousand: and finally, Mr. Eton . . . determines them to be an hundred and thirteen thousand four hundred. But the number of effective janizaries is best determined by the amount of their pay. Two thousand four hundred purses are issued every six months from the treasury; a sum which allows thirty piastres a man for an army calculated at forty thousand.[49]

The documentary sources have only partial information on the 1787–92 campaigns, but they do reveal a continuing trend. In early 1787, for example, 5750 cavalry and 2000 infantry were mobilized just for the army at the Ismail fortress, in exactly the manner described above, with the term '*miri*' persisting as meaning 'state-funded'.[50] Hence, though it was possible to prohibit the use of the term '*levend*' in official documents, the phenomenon of mobilizing the rural landless and lawless continued, and in the transition to a non-Janissary standing army, a plethora of names for such sources of manpower came into use, including the return of the term '*sekban*'.[51] The ethnicity of such troops was increasingly Albanian and Bosnian in the Balkans; Kurds and Caucasus tribal groups from Anatolia. In 1770 Albanians recruited as *miri levendat* were diverted on the way to the Danubian battlefront to quell the Morean rebellion. They also were called upon to reman the fortresses of the Danube and Black Sea following the war, and during the 1787–92 disasters, and later were one source of Selim III's *Nizam-i Cedid* troops. Provincial, non-Janissary *miri* troops had become the real army, in place of both Janissaries and *timariots*.[52]

In 1793–4, Selim III moved to create a small corps of soldiers (*asakir*) to be trained and disciplined in European fashion. He was responding to the advisers around him who made a series of recommendations on military reform: first and foremost, that a new budgetary regime be introduced; then, that a new core army be created from the young Muslim population of Anatolia, that it be trained by foreign officers, and that it be supported by mobile artillery corps. Rather than calling directly for the dissolution of the Janissaries, most reformers asserted the need to regain control over the *esame* lists, as it was an excuse for the maintenance of a completely outmoded military organization.[53] The most significant military official among the reformers was Koca Yusuf Pasha, grand vizier and commander-in-chief during most of the 1787–92 war. His recommendations recognized the necessity of organizing well trained, armed recruits (*tüfenkçi*, or 'musketeers'), both in the countryside under powerful provincial leaders, and in Istanbul, in barracks separated from the traditional corps. Others suggested that winter (peacetime) and summer (campaign) armies should be established, the former drawn from the Janissaries and the Balkans, the latter from the peasants of Anatolia.[54] Implicit in these reforms was a prototype conscript standing army and a reserve, with being a Muslim the prime condition of service. The extent of coercion is not spelled out. The first recruits for Selim III's experiment were renegades of the recent 1787–92 war and young men from the streets of Istanbul. Later, recruits came from Anatolia; they were housed in new, isolated barracks in Istanbul. By the time of Selim III's fall in 1807, the corps comprised upwards of 22,000 cavalry and infantrymen and almost 1600 officers, of whom half were in Istanbul and the Balkans, and the others in Anatolia.[55] The first, small corps of disciplined troops (perhaps 500) were important in the defeat of Napoleon's army at Acre in 1798.[56] Encouraged, Selim III furthered his *Nizam-i Cedid* agenda by extending recruitment for the new corps to the provinces, with command controlled by officers from Istanbul. At the same time, this initiative was strengthened by the new barracks in Üsküdar, which included a printing press, technical support and a hospital.[57] In 1802, Abdurrahman Pasha, governor of Karaman, and colonel of the *Nizam-i Cedid* regiments, one of the few of the independent provincial governors to take advantage of the access to power afforded by the new hierarchy of command, introduced a system of levies, and raised eight regiments himself. Provincial officials were to send specific numbers of recruits to Istanbul for a training period of six months to a year; half the recruits stayed in Istanbul, and half returned to their local militias. New barracks were built across Anatolia, and resistance seems to have been slight. Attempts to move the *Nizam-i Cedid* regiments into the Balkans, however, met with stiff resistance. In 1803–4, a rebellion in Rumelia and Bulgaria was put down by the new troops: one company of light artillery, a squadron of cavalry and three of the Karaman regiments, according to Saint-Denys.[58] The Balkans continued to resist the attempt to centralize the control of violence. In 1805, Abdurrahman Pasha attempted to conscript 20–25-year-olds from among the Janissaries and the villages of European Turkey. There was an immediate violent reaction, from Janissary and countryside alike, especially in Edirne in 1806.[59] Similar efforts led to the revolt of the fortresses of the Bosphorus by 1807 which brought down both Selim III and his *Nizam-i Cedid*. The failure was as much a result of Selim III's lack of spine, as of the new troops, who remained confined to their barracks by the sultan as the revolt unfolded.

When Mahmud II proclaimed the *Eşkinci* ordinance in May 1826 in his major initiative to reform the Janissaries, he introduced drill based on the new Egyptian model of Mehmed Ali, and called for a reform of the *esame*, the same persistent problem which had plagued Selim III. The ordinance received prior approval from the *şeyhülislam*, the empire's chief religious authority. The Janissaries' mutinous response to the public display of the new drill forced the issue and resulted in the dissolution of the corps on June 15 of that year.

Significantly, the courts martial that followed included a question to each prisoner: 'Are you a Janissary or Muslim?' By 20 June 1826, the 'Trained Victorious Muhammadan Soldiers', the core of the New Army, as it was called, numbering perhaps 2000, were assembled and paraded before the sultan.[60] The regulations were based on those of Selim III's *Nizam-i Cedid* army.[61] It was the beginning of the set of regulations that completely reformed the Ottoman military along European lines, and meant the imposition of both conscription and new taxes on the Muslim population. Because of strong resistance from both the veteran soldiers and the peoples of the Balkans, Mahmud II focused his conscription on the ranks of young Anatolians, especially in a levy *en masse* in 1828, justifying it as a holy war against the Russians. Islamic slogans were reiterated to convince, just as Orthodoxy in the Russian context remained a tool for troop encouragement, masking what had become a secularized institution.[62]

Rationalized conscription depended upon a census (1831), and an officer training school (1834). The significant problem remained mistrust of the nature and length of conscription (twelve years), and relationships between officers and the common soldier, as exemplified by the defeat at Nizib (1839), when even von Moltke acknowledged that the Ottomans had 'without doubt by far the best trained, best disciplined and best drilled [army] the Porte had ever put in the field.'[63] The Egyptian army under Ibrahim Pasha triumphed because of better command.

Of most interest, from the point of view of this chapter, was the creation in 1834 of the *redif*, conceived of as a national militia, or reserve corps, of every able-bodied Muslim man. Mahmud II's motives were twofold: to create a reserve force for the army for external uses and to further the imposition of central authority over eastern Anatolia, particularly over the rebellious Kurdish tribes.

Most arguments about the failure of the military reforms of Selim III and Mahmud II point to the imposition of new ideas from above, and to the Ottomans' inability to generate significant reform from within. I have argued the influence of the essential catalyst of control of external and internal violence, combined with certain social and cultural attributes of the Ottoman Empire, on the evolution of military mobilization. Clearly, the experience of a century of recruitment of *levendat*-style forces from the countryside, both Anatolia and the Balkans, contributed in no small way to the thinking of the advisers of Selim III, whose levies of *Nizam-i Cedid* troops drew most heavily from the Muslim population of Anatolia. Just as clearly Mahmud II, both building a new standing army and backing it up with province-wide *redifs*, based his new organization on the manpower and geographic range of his predecessors. His particular contribution lay in his firm commitment to the changes, as contrasted with Selim III, and in the calculated redefinition of holy war as the property of secularizing monarchy and its people, justifying modernization, and thereby delegitimizing the Janissaries as its icon, as exemplified in this excerpt from the *Eşkinci* ordinance:

> Vengeance, people of Muhammad, and you, zealous servants of this Ottoman monarchy which must last as long as the world, officers of all ranks, who are all faithful believers, defenders of the faith, friends of religion and glory, come unto us, let us unite our efforts to repair our breaches, and to raise up before our land the rampart of an army which is as trained as it is brave, and whose strokes directed by science, will travel far to attain their objective and to destroy the arsenal of military inventions of infidel Europe.[64]

Notes

1   Geoffrey Goodwin, *The Janissaries* (London, 1995); John Keegan, *History of Warfare* (New York, 1994), especially p. 182: 'Planted though it was in the capital city of the eastern Roman empire, the Topkapı remained a nomadic camp, where the horsetail standards of battle were processed before great men, and stables stood at the door.'

2   For example, see Charles Tilly, *Coercion, Capital and European States AD 990–1990* (Oxford, 1990), and 'States Making Wars Making States Making Wars', Jack Goldstone's review of that book in *Contemporary Sociology* 20 (1991), pp. 76–8.

3   Tallet, *War and Society in Early Modern Europe 1495–1715* (New York, 1992), p. 55, on the late seventeenth century.

4   G. Perjés, 'Army Provisioning, Logistics and Strategy in the Second Half of the 17th Century', *Acta Historica Academiae Scientiarum Hungaricae* 16 (1970), p. 11.

5   Jeremy Black, *European Warfare 1660–1815* (London, 1994), p. 98.

6   John A. Lynn, *Giant of the Grand Siècle: The French Army 1610–1715* (New York, 1997), pp. 4–9.

7   The decline of the *timar* system, the assignment of a fief in exchange for

military service, while related to a number of the issues discussed above, is beyond the purview of this chapter. *Timariot* soldiers were simply not present in any great numbers on the Danube in 1768.

8 Among the many editions of de Busbecq, E. Forster, ed., *Turkish Letters of Ogier de Busbecq* (Oxford, 1927) is often the most accessible.

9 Halil İnalcık with Donald Quataert, eds., *An Economic and Social History of the Ottoman Empire 1300–1914* (Cambridge, 1994), p. 659. On the Janissaries themselves, there is an appalling lack of systematic studies; Halil İnalcık, *The Ottoman Empire: The Classical Age, 1300–1600* (London, 1973), remains a useful introduction; H.A.R. Gibb and H. Bowen, *Islamic Society and the West*, vol. 1, pt. 1–2 (London, 1950–57), is a now very outdated study of Ottoman institutions. Goodwin's *The Janissaries*, a series of sensational anecdotes, purports to be a history of the corps.

10 Also called the Patrona Halil Revolt, after its leader. This 1730 revolt and, especially, another Janissary revolt of 1740 were also driven by the corps' resistance to campaigning in the east: dislike of fighting fellow Muslims was coupled with a dislike of the hardships, distance and deprivation, of that front.

11 İnalcık and Quataert, *Economic and Social History*, p. 716. How the system actually worked remains to be studied. The source for the figure of 400,000 is Baron de Tott, an eye-witness to the condition of the Ottoman forces in 1768.

12 Ignatius Mouradgea D'Ohsson, *Tableau général de l'Empire othoman* (7 vols., Paris, 1788–1821), vol. 7, pp. 337–9. D'Ohsson distinguishes between a pay ticket (*memhur*) and a ration ticket (*esame*), but most sources refer most often to *esame*. He also mentions the government's attempts at intervention, including an amusing conversation between the agha of the Janissaries and Mustafa III (1757–74) in which the agha informs him that the Janissaries received only half of the quarterly pay, while the rest passed into the houses of the ulema, the ministers of the state and the officers of the palace.

13 Jucherau de Saint-Denys, *Révolutions de Constantinople en 1807 et 1808* (2 vols., Paris, 1829), vol. 1, p. 49.

14 William C. Fuller, *Strategy Power in Russia, 1600–1914* (New York, 1992), p. 105.

15 John L.H. Keep, *Soldiers of the Tsar: Army and Society in Russia 1462–1874* (Oxford, 1985), p. 88.

16 Ibid., p. 107.

17 Richard Ungermann, *Der russisch–türkische Krieg 1768–1774* (Vienna: 1906), p. 232.

18 Black, *European Warfare*, p. 122.

19 Keep, *Soldiers of the Tsar*, p. 155.

20 These topics are treated at some length in Fuller and Keep as regards the Russians. Black tackles the topic for the more general European arena. The

discussion of losses on the march is from Christopher Duffy, *Russia's Military Way to the West* (London, 1981), pp. 126–9.

21 Tallett suggests that a 25 per cent loss-rate of all men under arms was standard in the seventeenth-century French army (Tallet, *War and Society*, p. 105).

21 Sadullah Enverî, *Tarih* (1780), Istanbul University MS T 5994, fos. 328v–329.

22 Süleyman şemdanizade, *Mür'i't-Tevârih*, ed. M. Münir Aktepe (4 vols., Istanbul, 1980), vol. 2 (B), pp. 59–61.

23 İnalcık, 'Military and Fiscal Transformation in the Ottoman Empire, 1600–1700', *Archivum Ottomanicum* 6 (1980), p. 292; Mustafa Cezar, *Osmanlı Tarihinde Levendler* (Istanbul, 1965), pp. 351–6.

24 İnalcık, 'Military and Fiscal Transformation', p. 295. '*Levend*' is an elastic term, with other meanings, such as 'bandit' or 'outlaw', in the period under discussion. It is also used for 'marine' in the navy.

25 Cezar, *Osmanlı Tarihinde Levendler*, pp. 214–16; also d'Ohsson, *Tableau général de l'Empire othoman*, vol. 7, p. 381ff. Such terms had replaced all earlier names for locally raised forces, such as *yaya*, *müsellem*, *azab* and *yürük*; latterly, *sarıca* and *sekban* also fell out of use, though *sekban* (also *segban* or *seymen*) was retained in the Janissaries as a regimental division (d'Ohsson, *Tableau général de l'Empire othoman*, vol. 7, p. 308).

26 Cezar, *Osmanlı Tarihinde Levendler*, p. 289; İnalcık, 'Military and Fiscal Transformation', p. 295.

27 İnalcık with Quataert, *Economic and Social History*, p. 659.

28 İnalcık, 'Military and Fiscal Transformation', pp. 301, 307–8. Karen Barkey, *Bandits and Bureaucrats: The Ottoman Route to State Centralization* (Ithaca, 1994), develops this theme.

29 This was noted by Ahmed Resmi in 1769. See Virginia H. Aksan, *An Ottoman Statesman in War and Peace: Ahmed Resmi Efendi, 1700–1783* (Leiden, 1995), p. 136.

30 D'Ohsson, *Tableau général de l'Empire othoman*, vol. 7, p. 382.

31 The evidence for these assertions comes from a register and account book devoted exclusively to the mobilization of the *miri levendat*: Prime Minister's Archives, Maliyeden Müdevver Collection (hereafter MM) 4683, various pages. This remarkable record includes both the source of recruits and where they were being sent. See Virginia H. Aksan, 'Whatever Happened to the Janissaries?', *War in History*, 5 (1998), pp. 23–36, for a micro-study of the register.

32 Cezar, *Osmanlı Tarihinde Levendler*, p. 308.

33 MM 6111, fo. 2, and repeated on fo. 18. This particular register is full of other provincial troops, and also notes the reorganizing of Janissary regiments and garrisons throughout eastern Anatolia.

34 One Ottoman source recorded that 400,000 men and animals assembled in Bender in 1769 (Sadullah Enveri, *Tarih*, Istanbul University MS T 5994,

dated 1780, fos. 8v and 22v–24). A roll call of Janissaries from early 1771 listed a total of 62,611, though a year later half that number were struck from the list (MM 17383). This figure is suspect, as the long period (1771–3) of truce and negotiation was then under way.

35 Mustafa Kesbi, *İbretnüma-yi Devlet*, Süleymaniye Library, Ali Amiri Collection MS 484, fo. 35v.

36 Ibid., fo. 35.

37 D'Ohsson, *Tableau général de l'Empire othoman*, vol. 7, pp. 381–2.

38 See Aksan, 'Whatever Happened to the Janissaries?', for more details.

39 Prime Minister's Archives, Mühimme Collection, defter 167, fo. 25.

40 The example used here is Prime Minister's Archives, Cevdet Askeriye Collection 18671, from September 1770, which is reproduced in Cezar, *Osmanlı Tarihinde Levendler*, pp. 443–4. He considers 1737 as the date of the regular appearance of such officers of rank and file as *yüzbaşı* (captain) and *binbaşı* (major), p. 360. For more details, see Aksan, 'Whatever Happened to the Janissaries?'.

41 The first figure is based on calculations from the appendices in Yuzo Nagata, *Muhsinzâde Mehmed Paşa ve Âyânlık Müessesesi* (Tokyo, 1976); the second is from Saint-Denys, *Révolutions de Constantinople*, vol. 1, p. 92.

42 Cezar, *Osmanlı Tarihinde Levendler*, pp. 353–4.

43 D'Ohsson, *Tableau général de l'Empire othoman*, vol. 7 pp. 345–6. The Janissaries in Constantinople were not allowed to bear arms during peacetime. He adds that, once distributed, the weapons would never be seen again.

44 See Gabor Agoston, 'Ottoman Artillery and European Military Technology in the Fifteenth and Seventeenth Centuries, *Acta Orientalia Academiae Scientiarum Hungaricae* 47 (1994), pp. 15–48, and 'Gunpowder for the Sultan's Army: New Sources on the Supply of Gunpowder to the Ottoman Army in the Hungarian Campaigns of the Sixteenth and Seventeenth Centuries', *Turcica* 25 (1993), pp. 75–96; also Saint-Denys, *Révolutions de Constantinople*, vol. 1, p. 66; and Virginia H. Aksan, 'Baron de Tott's *"Wretched Fanaticks"* and Ottoman Military Reform in the Late Eighteenth Century', unpublished paper.

45 şemdanizade, *Mür'i't-Tevârih*, vol. 2 (B), p. 12.

46 See Prime Minister's Archives, Bab-ı Defter, Baş Muhasebe Kalemi (hereafter D.BşM), Ordu Hazinesi (Army Treasury) Collection (ORH) dosya 48, gömlek 91, dated July 1769, a formula for that office; D.BşM 4250, p. 8, dated June 1771, for a detailed cavalryman's account; Duffy, *Russia's Military Way to the West*, p. 131, for the Russian side.

47 Cezar, *Osmanlı Tarihinde Levendler*, p. 307. The tactic was previously tried on the far smaller *sekban* organization in 1718; Cezar, *Osmanlı Tarihinde Levendler*, pp. 303–5. Such names persist as part of the military ethos long after their organizational function has been superseded.

48 MM 4683, pp. 578–9.

49 Thomas Thornton, *The Present State of Turkey* (London, 1807), pp. 173–4. Even Stanford Shaw's *Between Old and New: The Ottoman Empire under Sultan Selim III, 1789–1807* (Cambridge, MA., 1971) does not include recruitment numbers for that war. James Porter's *Observations on the Religion, Law, Government and Manners of the Turks* was published in London in 1768. Peyssonnel and de Tott were both French consuls to the Ottoman court, and authors of studies of the Ottomans; de Tott's *Memoirs of Baron de Tott*, published in English and French in 1785–6, was a European best-seller; Eton's famous diatribe against the Turks, *A Survey of the Turkish Empire* (London, 1798), long served as a major source of information for nineteenth-century European historians. A close study of the Ottoman archives such as I pursued for the 1768 war needs to be undertaken for all the subsequent confrontations of the pre-Tanzimat period.

50 MM 4683, pp. 885–7. In point of fact, the term '*Ismail ordusu*' ('Ismail army') represents a new departure in the Ottoman documents, perhaps a recognition of various fronts requiring smaller armies. Similarly, the term '*sefer-i hümayun*' ('imperial campaign') has disappeared. These are straightforward military orders, couched in the formulas described above.

51 Cezar, *Osmanlı Tarihinde Levendler*, pp. 297, 314, notes that *sekban, sarıca, levend, deli* ('crazy'), and *gönüllü* ('volunteer'), among others, were all in circulation at the time.

52 Yuzo Nagata, *Studies on the Social and Economic History of the Ottoman Empire* (Izmir, 1997), p. 111, in a chapter based on his dissertation and called 'The Greek Rebellion of 1770 in the Morea Peninsula'; fuller information is to be found in his *Muhsinzâde Mehmed Paşa*. The new regiments of Mustafa Bayraktar Pasha, organized at the same time as those of Selim III, were called *Sekban-ı Cedid*. (Cezar, *Osmanlı Tarihinde Levendler*, p. 115).

53 İnalcık with Quataert, *Economic and Social History*, pp. 966–70. While Shaw's work discusses the reformers and their agendas in a general way, the actual reform documents have yet to be published, analyzed and discussed in any real systematic fashion. The texts themselves are available in summarizd form in modern Turkish, in Enver Ziya Karal, 'Nizâm-ı Cedid'e Dâir Lâyihalar', *Tarih Vesikaları* 1 (1941–2), pp. 414–25, and 2 (1942–3), pp. 104–11, 342–51, 424–32.

54 Shaw, *Between Old and New*, pp. 100–101; but he likens the new troops to the *devşirme* system. In that he is mistaken: the reformers abandoned any idea of using enslaved or otherwise tributary non-Muslims in these new armies.

55 Shaw, *Between Old and New*, pp. 130–32; see also Mahmud Raif Efendi, *Osmanlı İmparatorluğu'nda Yeni Nizamların Cedveli* (Istanbul, 1988).

56 Saint-Denys, *Révolutions de Constantinople*, vol. 1, pp. 92–5, and vol. 2, pp. 12–13.

57 See Kemal Beydilli's monumental study on the technical support, schooling and publishing of the period, *Türk Bilim ve Matbaacılık Tarihinde Mühendishâne, Mühendishâne Matbaası ve Kütüphanesi (1776–1826)* (Istanbul, 1995).

58 Saint-Denys, *Révolutions de Constantinople*, vol. 2, pp. 24–5; Shaw, *Between Old and New*, p. 132.

59 Saint-Denys, *Révolutions de Constantinople*, vol. 2, pp. 26–9.

60 Howard Reed's description of this, 'The Destruction of the Janissaries by Mahmud II in June 1826', PhD thesis (Princeton University, 1951), remains useful. I have consulted here Max Gross, 'Military Reform in the Ottoman Empire: The Military Reforms of Sultan Mahmud II (1808–1839)', MA thesis (American University of Beirut, 1971), which made extensive use of Reed's work. Of course, asking the Janissary that question was equally prompted by the attempt to eliminate the heretical Bektaşi influence. The result was the same. See also Avigdor Levy, 'Military Problem of Centralization in the Ottoman Empire in the Eighteenth Century', *Middle Eastern Studies* 18 (1982), pp. 227–49, and 'The Officer Corps in Sultan II's New Ottoman Army, 1826–39', *International Journal of Middle East Studies* 2 (1971), pp. 21–39.

61 Gross, 'Military Reform', p. 193, compared the two.

62 Keep, *Soldiers of the Tsar*, pp. 205–6. The famous Suvorov exhorted his troops to 'Die for the Virgin, for your mother the Empress, for the royal family' (Philip Longworth, *The Art of Victory: The Life and Achievements of Generalissimo Suvorov, 1729–1800* (London, 1965), p. 217). The original Russian has 'mother' only, referring either to Russia or to Catherine II.

63 Gross, 'Military Reform', p. 211.

64 Gross, 'Military reform', p. 233, as translated by Howard Reed.

2· The Manning of the Ottoman Navy in the Heyday of Sail (1660–1850)

Daniel Panzac

Settled upon three continents, the Ottoman Empire was a huge political organization gathering together a large number of peoples and presenting a great variety of languages, religions, cultures and traditions. In spite of this heterogeneity, the empire remained largely intact from the end of the sixteenth century to the beginning of the nineteenth. Of course, the sultan, the Islamic religion, the administration and the army were strong factors of cohesion, but during the seventeenth century the empire also became a large economic market, a 'world economy', according to Fernand Braudel, which contributed strongly to keeping together the different parts of it. The eastern basin of the Mediterranean was the core of the empire and the Black Sea, completely surrounded by Ottoman territories, was virtually a Turkish lake. The Ottoman leaders were aware of the importance of the seas and did their best, through the centuries, to maintain a strong navy in order to keep maritime links free and open within the empire.

A navy has two main components: ships in fighting order and men able to use them. This chapter is devoted to the latter, which is of course the most important; ships are mentioned only when they influenced the manning of the navy. For two centuries, from the 1660s, which saw the end of the galleys, to the 1850s when the armoured steam-powered battleship came to the fore, the sailing-vessel was, as elsewhere, the capital ship of the Ottoman navy.

From the galley oarsman to the sailing-vessel's able seaman

The research of a Turkish scholar in the archives of Istanbul enables us to gain a precise idea of the crews of the Ottoman navy during the War of Crete (1645–69).[1] According to the objectives formulated by the sultan's Council of State, the Kapudan Pasha (Grand Admiral) decided on the number of galleys to be commissioned each year and on the number of men to be recruited to serve on them. For the year 1660–61 (1071 AH), the navy had fifty-six galleys to put to sea, each of them with a complement consisting of sailors (*bahriler*), oarsmen (*kürekçiler*) and soldiers, especially gunners (*topçular*), Janissaries (*yeniçeriler*) and iron-sides (*cebeliler*). We do not know the precise number of sailors charged with the management of the lateen sails and the rudder, but on the basis of a comparison with European galleys, which were quite similar to the Ottoman ones, and which needed 25 to 30 men for the same purpose, we can estimate that a total of 1200 to 1500 sailors was required for the navy in that year.

The oarsmen constituted the main part of the crews and recruiting them each year was the main concern of the Kapudan Pasha. For 1660, the document reckoned with a requirement of 12,391 oarsmen, or an average of 221 for each galley. The recruitment included 835 convicts (6.6 per cent), while the others (93.49 per cent) were free men. This was definitely very different from the Christian navies, which used almost exclusively convicts and slaves. The free oarsmen generally received 3000 akçe (or aspers) for the yearly campaign, which ordinarily lasted around six months, at 15 to 20 akçe per day. Several means were used to recruit them.

There were 4441 (35.8 per cent) volunteers. Pay and other expenses, mainly catering, were assessed at 6000 akçe for each man, which was obtained by a specific tax, the *bedel* (payment-in-lieu). In the capital, Istanbul, two social groups had to support a certain number of oarsmen by paying this tax to the *kadı* (judge). The first group was the non-Muslim communities: in 1660, the Jewish community was charged with a payment equivalent to 150 oarsmen, the Greeks with an equivalent to 125 and the Armenians with one equalling 100. The second group was the guilds (*esnaf*), which had to support 869 oarsmen. The innkeepers (*meyhaneciler*) supported 248, the boatsmen (*peremeciler*) 110, porters (*hammallar*) 40, and so on. Altogether, Istanbul supported 1244 oars-men, one-tenth of the navy in 1660.

The main portion of the oarsmen was provided by the provinces, according to two different systems. The first called for a *bedel* of 28 mil-lions akçe to be levied on the inner Anatolian provinces, those furthest from the shore. The second was a sharing-out system which provided 5068 men: provinces, and sometimes districts, had to send men according to the number of their households. Owing to the reluctance of the men who were called to serve in this way, a third means, much more brutal, was used to fill the – always incomplete – ranks of the oarsmen: patrols of soldiers were sent out with orders to arrest all men who seemed able to row on the galleys. This exactly recalls the contemporary European press-gangs.

In fact, the geographical origins of the oarsmen were quite restricted.

Table 1: Origins of Oarsmen in 1660–61

Province	Militia	Pressed	Total
Aydın	644	—	644
Saruhan	456	230	686
Menteşe	447	—	447
Siğla	433	—	433
Hamidili	153	90	243
Karası	221	120	341
Biga	131	70	201
Teke	108	60	168
Alaye	29	17	46
Kütahya	307	205	512
Hüdavendigâr	359	450	809
Karahisar	7	46	53
Ankara	144	90	234
Sultanönü	31	31	
Çankırı	110	70	180
Bolu	501	310	811
Kastamonu	322	210	532
District			
Edirne	244	300	544
Bursa	338	—	338
Gelibolu	8	—	82
Evreşe	27	—	27
Kandıra	5	—	5
Total	5,068	2,299	7,367

Apart from the 15 per cent recruited from the districts of Edirne and Gelibolu located in European Turkey, close to Istanbul, nearly all the oarsmen came from western Anatolia, with a small contingent from central Anatolia. As is to be expected, fully 71.4 per cent hailed from the coastal provinces, which were the most densely inhabited areas and which were closest to the arsenal of Istanbul. Some of the men were sent to the harbours of Izmit, Izmir and Rhodes, which were in use during the Cretan War, rather than to Istanbul.

The soldiers included four or five gunnners per ship, which was a small number but there were only three to five guns on a galley and these specialist troops served as chief gunners and were assisted by the other soldiers. In 1660, 1975 Janissaries were nominated to serve with the navy, an average of thirty-five per galley; five hundred armoured soldiers, eight to ten per ship also served on board. Soldiers in each of these groups received, besides their ordinary pay, an extra pay of 4 to 5 akçe per day.

The Ottoman galley, like the Christian one, was a standard ship, which boarded about three hundred men (220 oarsmen, 30 sailors and 50 soldiers). In use in the Ottoman navy since the fifteenth century without any important change, this type of ship was suddenly challenged and quickly replaced in the last third of the seventeenth century by the sailing-vessel, which sat high above the sea, was usually square-rigged, was moved only by the wind and was heavily armed with guns.

The new Ottoman navy

During the Cretan War, the Ottomans became aware of the superiority of the Venetian sailing-vessels over their own galleys. Apart from a few merchantmen hired from the Europeans, the Ottomans had no vessels similar to the Venetian ones. In the early 1680s, the Grand Vizier, Merzifonlu Kara Mustafa, asked the North African corsairs for information about this type of ship, which they had used for a long time. It was probably the North Africans who suggested taking on a shipbuilder from Leghorn (a convert to Islam) who, in 1682, launched the first Ottoman sailing-vessel in the arsenal of Istanbul.[2] In 1684, six vessels were commissioned and ten were on the slips. Under the energetic and efficient leadership of Grand Admiral Hüseyn Mezzamorto (1695–1701), an Algerian, the Ottomans commissioned fifteen to twenty vessels each year.[3] These efforts were continued later, during the Second Morean War (1714–18) when the Ottomans put twenty to twenty-five vessels to sea each year. Twenty years later, the Ottoman navy was much more impressive, at least on paper, with thirty-three vessels. But as in the previous century only a part of the fleet was commissioned each year: for example, in 1740, eight vessels made a cruise in the Aegean Sea during the summer.[4] This new Ottoman navy had three main characteristics.

First, the progressive withdrawal of the galleys meant that their number fell to fifteen in 1701. It remained at this level until the 1760s, before they disappeared altogether during the following years. In the eighteenth century, their duties were restricted to scouting, patrolling the coasts and the islands of the Aegean and sometimes towing the sailing-vessels.

Second, the growth in number of the sailing-ships was accompanied by a growth in their size and in the strength of their complements. The crew of the 1690 flagship consisted of 418 men: it reached 601 in 1699[5] and 1470 in 1738.[6]

Table 2: The Ottoman Navy in 1699 and 1738

Complement	1699	1738
1500	—	1
1300	—	1
1100	—	1
1000	—	1
800	—	6
750	—	5
650	—	4
600	1	—
500	—	1
450	—	7
400	2	3
350	3	1
300	8	1
250	3	1
200	3	—
Total	20	33

In 1699, except for the flagship, which had 600 men on board, all the vessels had between 200 and 400 men. In full commission, the 20 vessels needed 6000 men. Under the same circumstances, the 33 vessels of 1738 needed 21,800 men, three and half times as many. In fact, according to the standards of just thirty years later, only the flagship of 1699 would still be classed as a first-rate vessel.

Third, we have seen how limited was the number of different tasks on a galley, which makes for a spectacular contrast with the great number of different duties and functions on board a sailing-vessel. Managing a sailing-ship, which often had to be sailed and fought simultaneously, was a very complicated matter, and needed a great number of skilled men. In 1690, the 418 men of the flagship had 18 separate occupations, which number increased to 40 over the following years.[7] We can get a picture of the manning of an Ottoman sailing-vessel thanks to the detailed lists of duties existing for the flagships of 1699, 1738 and 1815.[8] These huge men-of-war each had 600–800 men on board in 1699, 1470 in 1738 and 1207 in 1815. The different occupations can be grouped under more general functions:

- Steering. In 1699, we find ten quarterdeck officers (reis), two chief helmsmen (serdümen) and eighteen pilots (dümen). In 1738, the staff counted eight officers, assisted by twenty-two pilots and helmsmen. In 1815, six officers were charged with the steering with thirty petty officers (rüesayı rubul'u) and six officers were occupied with the sails (gabayyaran-ı çamlıca) with thirty-one able seamen.

- Administration and victualling. In 1699, six persons under the purser (hoca) were busy in this field, and they were assisted by several storekeepers (vekil-i harc, anbarcı). There were seven in 1738 and thirteen in 1815, of whom five were pursers.

- Gunnery. The staff was of five men, including the chief gunner (birinci topçu başı); there were exactly the same number in 1699, 1738 and 1815.

- Craftsmen. There was one first carpenter (başmarangoz) with three mates; the same breakdown was noted for the caulkers (kalafat) in 1699 and 1738. In 1815, nine carpenters were found, as well as eight caulkers and five sailmakers (badbânî).

- Souls and bodies. The flagship of 1699 had one imam and one surgeon (cerrah) on board. In 1738, two imams were assisted by two others and there was also one surgeon. In 1815, there was one imam, one doctor and one surgeon.

- Longboat crews. One coaxwain (sandal reisi) and forty oarsmen were listed in 1699, three coaxwains in 1738 and two with forty-eight oarsmen in 1815.

- Marines (*levendler*). These were 5 officers in 1699, with 200 men under their command; 9 officers and 350 men in 1738 and 10 officers, with no precise data on the number of men under their command, in 1815.

- Sailors. In 1699, there were 498 all together: 200 were able seamen (*aylakcılar*); 200 could help with the handling of the sails but were mainly gunners (*topçular*), and 98 were supply sailors (*saatçılar*). In 1738, the flagship had 1020 sailors on board (no breakdown is given), and in 1815 we know only that there were 897 marines and sailors.

The marines were engaged for the whole year, and after the end of the campaign they had to guard the ships that were laid up for the winter, living either on board or in barracks built for them in 1718 by Süleyman Kapudan Pasha on the outskirts of the capital, in Eyüp, Üsküdar and Beşiktaş. They were mainly Muslim but some were Greeks, who were distinguished by their dress and turban. Among the sailors there were Muslims but also Greeks and even Armenians. All had the same pay in 1738 as they had had half a century before: 16 to 18 akçe per day. They were recruited according to the same system and in the same provinces as in the century before for the oarsmen. They were gathered in in the ward of Kasımpaşa on the Golden Horn before the fleet left Istanbul and they were infamous for their brawls and violence.

The lack of change in the number of duties and the number of men assigned to them over the space of a century and half is remarkable. In fact, beyond a certain size, a big sailing-vessel needed roughly the same complement as a smaller one; only the number of soldiers varied. The professional staff of the three ships, including the craftsmen, represented around a hundred men. By contrast, the total number of marines and sailors was around 700 in 1699, 1400 in 1738 and over 1000 in 1815.

I would stress the speed and efficiency of the Ottoman navy in adapting to the new conditions created by the appearance of the sailing-vessel. The importance of this change was recognized as early as 1682 with the building of the first Ottoman sailing-warship. That year, several imperial edicts were promulgated which regulated the recruitment and organization of the sailors and marines, as well as the creation of a new kind of admiral: the *Kapudane* (Grand Admiral). He held first rank in command of the sailing-vessels, just behind the Kapudan Pasha, and before the two other admirals, the *Patrona* and the *Riyale*, whose commands were linked to the squadrons of galleys. At great cost, in less than fifteen years the navy was able to change its oarsmen into sailors, to give up Janissaries and ironsides and replace them with marines, and to create a new body of naval officers and petty officers. The general level of knowledge and ability was probably low but high enough to handle the ships competently. In the First Morean War (1685–99), the Venetian squadrons ruled the Aegean sea, beat the Ottoman fleet at the Dardanelles and severed communications between the coastal Ottoman provinces,[9] but during the Second Morean War (1714–18), the Ottoman navy played a decisive role during the reconquest of the Morea and several times successfully challenged the Venetian navy at the mouth of the Adriatic.

The Ottoman navy: An unlucky but obstinate phoenix (1770–1850)

Except for some small and limited interventions in the Black Sea in 1738–9, the Ottoman navy did not see any military action for half a century, from 1718 to 1769, when the war with Russia started. A long period of wars then began for the Ottoman Empire. Between 1769 and 1841, the empire was involved in nine wars lasting a total of twenty-nine years, during which the Mediterranean and the Black Sea were often decisive battlefields but where the Ottoman squadrons frequently suffered heavy defeats. Because of its prominent role, the Ottoman state did its best, after each defeat, to reconstruct the navy by looking to modernize both the material and the crews. The urgency of the situation drove the Ottoman Empire to call on European technicians for help. Their interventions were an important part of the general involvement of Europe in the empire at the same time.

Çeşme: The revelation of Ottoman weaknesses

On 6 July 1770, the Ottoman navy, under the orders of Hüsamettin Kapudan Pasha, was destroyed by the Russian fleet led by the brothers Orlov in the bay of Çeşme: 11 ships of the line, 6 frigates, 6 three-masters, 7 galleys and 32 other small craft were burnt while one sailing-vessel and 5 galleys were captured. Out of 15,000 to 17,000 men, 5000 to 6000 were killed, wounded or captured. For half a century, the Ottoman Empire had been convinced that its navy, which had successfully challenged Venice in 1714–18, would always be able to withstand any enemy bold enough to enter the Aegean. The disaster of Çeşme revealed brutally the weaknesses and shortcomings in the Ottoman navy. These are made explicit in a French source of 1806:

Not long ago Turkish vessels were extraordinarily high above the waterline, especially the poop, which was really disproportionate. These ships were at the mercy of the wind: they were heavy in all their movements, always drifting and very vulnerable to squalls; finally, during battles they offered a large target to the enemy cannonballs. Their headway was ponderous and their going-about very slow because their manoeuvres were untidy and lacked precision. Inside, Turkish vessels were big and roomy, built of oak, but the hulls were weak owing to the distance between the main timbers . . . They did not last long and soon started leaking in spite of the most careful caulking. The artillery consisted of copper guns but [they were] of unequal calibre and their deployment was awkward and slow. The decks were all cleared very slowly and with much disorder.[10]

The Ottoman vessel, short, broad and rising high above the waterline, was nothing but the European model in use at the end of the seventeenth century, as it had been copied by the Ottomans at that time.[11] Traditionalism, induced by the lack of any battle for more than fifty years, weighed heavily upon the men. Almost all contemporary witnesses point out the incompetence and bribery reigning among the officers and the bullying and ignorance among the sailors and marines. The recruiting-system had not changed for a century. But the dismissal of the sailors in October and their replacement by newcomers the following April deprived the navy of a permanent body of trained sailors. Moreover, the pay was the same for practically a century, while the Ottoman currency suffered serious devaluation and the difficulties of the Ottoman Treasury meant that the navy was often unable to secure regular payment.

Where the officers were concerned, the situation was probably worse. As almost all of them had risen from the ranks, the nautical knowledge they possessed seems to have been very slight. This caused the problems with the manoeuvres observed at the start of the campaign which ended at Çeşme. There were also aggravating circumstances. The naval officers, like all Ottoman officials, bought their place and looked to make a return on their investment beyond their pay. The captains were in charge of buying supplies for their crews but, in spite of inspections, they cheated on the real number of their men and kept for themselves the money supposedly spent on their imaginary sailors. With the bought agreement of their commanders, they used their ships for merchant shipping. Such slack behaviour, though without serious consequences in peacetime, brought disaster in wartime. The Ottoman government was perfectly aware of this and did its best to restore the navy.

The time of the great Kapudan Pashas (1774–1807)

After the imperial edicts of 1682, which were linked to the adoption of the sailing-vessel, the organization of the navy remained largely unchanged. From 1770 onwards, the Ottoman state launched a policy of faster reforms in which two Kapudan Pashas played a prominent role, Gazi Hasan Pasha (1774–90) and Küçük Hüseyn Pasha (1792–1803). Their personalities and their determination to strengthen the navy once more were strongly supported by the Sultans, Abdülhamid I (1774–89) and especially Selim III (1789–1807),[12] who gave them the opportunity to act for a long time (sixteen and eleven years respectively) in a job where the turnover was usually fast. Their reforms partly lasted after their deaths, unlike what happened to the reforms in the army after Selim III's death. The first task was to build new ships to replace the ones destroyed. Aware of the defects of the old fleet, the Ottomans now called for French engineers. From 1789 to 1798, forty-five new large warships, ships of the line and frigates, all of modern design, were brought into service. The Ottoman state was soon able to put twenty to twenty-five large vessels and a dozen frigates to sea each year. During the same period, the government had to deal with the fearsome problem of the manning of this new fleet.

Küçük Hüseyn Pasha undertook deeper reforms, which were announced in July 1792 through the promulgation of several imperial firmans. The hierarchy of the officers was reorganized with new pay based, officially, on competence and no longer on nepotism and bribery. As the promotions in the future had to be granted according to the quality and the knowledge of the officers, teaching and training them became crucial. The Ottomans looked for a school which was able to train shipbuilding engineers and navy officers together. The first attempt, conducted by Gazi Hasan Pasha in 1784–8, was based on French engineers on duty in Istanbul, but the school failed when the French left. The first new school was really established in 1795 in the Arsenal, once more under the guidance of a Frenchman, Le Brun, but with a staff of Ottoman teachers.[13] It consisted of two sections: ten pupils in naval architecture and twenty in navigation, with mathematics common to both sections. Teaching continued for three years after a preparatory year. In 1805, the navy section had about forty pupils, all Muslims because there were no Christian officers in the navy. They earned a monthly pay of 24 kuruş; twenty-four of them were at school and eleven trainees were on board warships. The pay of the officers improved, as is shown by the following table:

Table 3: Yearly Pay in the Ottoman Navy 1738—1805 (in legal kurus)

Grade	1738	1792	1805
Kapudane	6000	7500	12,500
Liman reisi		6000	12,500
Patrona	4500	6000	10,000
Riyale	3000	5000	9000
Flagship captain	2000	2433	
Captain of a three-decker	1000	1500	4500
1st rank captain	1000	2500	4000
2nd rank captain		2350	3000
1st rank frigate captain		1850	2500
2nd rank frigate captain		1600	2250
1st rank flagship lieut.	350	1250	1500
1st lieut. 1st-rate ship	270	833	1150
1st lieut. 2nd-rate ship	180	783	1000

Of course, these data have to be used with care but we can note that in 1792 the pay of the junior officers was raised much more than that of the senior officers. In 1805, all pay was raised in order to make up for inflation.

The recruiting system for the rank and file had not changed. A list of 144 officers in 1800 gives the places of birth for one hundred of them: Aegean isles and coasts, sixteen; Crete, eighteen; Albanian coast, twenty-three; Istanbul, twelve; Pontic Anatolia, nine; inner Anatolia, three; Marmara coasts, three; Maghrib, four; Egypt, nine; Other places, three.

Since nearly all the officers were taken from the ranks, the places of birth listed here faithfully reflect those of the sailors themselves. We notice that 72 per cent of the men came from the Mediterranean and its adjoining seas, the Marmara and Adriatic, that is to say, the same percentage as in the 1660s. Moreover, a significant part was provided by

Egypt and the Maghreb. The incompetence of the sailors who were newly recruited each spring suggested to Gazi Hasan Pasha that a few thousand sailors should be recruited for several years. He wanted to build new barracks for them in Istanbul in order to obtain trained men who would then be able to become petty officers for the annual levies. But, fearing that the Kapudan Pasha would have at his disposal a body of devoted military men, the other viziers saw to it that this idea came to nothing. The idea was taken up by Küçük Hüseyn Pasha, and a body of 3000 professional sailors was organized and settled in new barracks in the Arsenal of Istanbul. For them, too, pay was linked to inflation: the daily wages of a sailor, which had been 16 to 18 akçe for a century, was raised to between 30 and 40 akçe in 1792 and reached 160 akçe for professional and volunteer sailors in 1805.

A significant change appeared in the way the men were allocated to different duties: from now on, only Muslims were appointed marines and gunners, while the Greeks were charged solely with navigation duties. This decision resulted from the Greek insurrection in the Morea provoked by the Russians in 1770. Of course, this was not the first rebellion in the Ottoman Empire but it was the first supported by a foreign state which had not only a religious but also a kind of nationalistic aspect.

In order to improve the levy system, a small body of specialized officers (*lonca başı*) was created whose duty it was to supervise the recruiting areas in Anatolia, Rumelia, Crete, Cyprus and the sancak of Alanya.

A special Marine Corps of 1000 men, similar to the army's *Nizam-i Cedid*, was created in two regiments under the command of a *Tüfekçi Kapudanı*. These men had to be able to serve both on shore and on board, to handle the guns and to rig the sails.

The growth of the navy under Abdülhamid I and Selim III had three main characteristics.

First, after a century of structural immobility, the navy was reorganized and had to assimilate a number of innovations, notably in its personnel. Owing to the confusion and rivalries reigning between the different services, in particular between the *Kapudane* and the *Tersane Emini* (Director of the Arsenal), the government created a Ministry of the Navy, the Bahriye Nezareti, which was at the head of the entire hierarchy and which symbolized the renewal of the navy.

Second, great efforts were made to improve the number and ability of professionals, both among officers and among the men.

Third, the quarter-century after the defeat at Çeşme saw the regeneration of the Ottoman navy, with squadrons which were very active both in the Mediterranean and in the Black Sea. In 1787–91, the Ottoman navy was able, in the Black Sea, if not to defeat, at least to challenge and, sometimes, to thwart the Russian navy. Bonaparte's expedition in Egypt brought about a reversal of the alliances in 1798–1801: Ottoman warships cooperated with Russian and English squadrons against Corfu and Ancona, which were occupied by French troops; Ottoman warships also made possible the transport and landing of an Ottoman army in Egypt.

The navy during the early Tanzimat (1845–8)

After eight years of quiet which followed the peace signed with Russia at Jassy in 1812, the Ottoman navy had to face the Greek insurrection in 1820. The importance of the islanders among the rebels and the role and activity of their ships compelled the Ottoman navy to wage a kind of war which had little to do with the classical squadron battles which involved heavy sailing-vessels. Neither the Ottoman warships nor their crews were fit to face this naval guerrilla war imposed on them by the Greek seamen. After numerous setbacks, the Ottomans succeeded in countering the Greek attacks, in holding them in check and then in partly restoring the efficiency and the prestige of the navy. The disaster of Navarino in October 1827 inflicted by a combined British, French and Russian squadron put everything back into question. Restored once more during the following years, the navy had to face the Egyptian navy of Mehmed Ali during the years 1830–40. It was during great international difficulties and with acute shortage of money that the Ottoman navy had to solve material problems and to completely reorganize its manning owing to the Greek upheaval and its consequences.

Several documents, Ottoman and European, give us a pretty good idea of the Ottoman navy during the 1840s. The empire was at peace and the threat of Mehmed Ali had passed, thanks to the European Powers.

Recruitment

For centuries, the Ottoman navy had found the majority of the men, Muslims and Christians, in the Mediterranean coastal provinces from where they had to join warships for a six month campaign. After more than two centuries, this system was completely transformed.

From 1820 onwards, the Greeks disappeared from Ottoman warships and the navy had to replace them with Muslims. However, the increase of the Egyptian navy and the French conquest of Algiers deprived the Ottoman Empire of important Muslim recruiting-areas for sailors and the need for men was so strong that from 1835 on the navy called on Christians again: 1098 that year and 1491 in 1837. Documents are lacking from then until 1845, when 142 were listed. The levy in 1851, foresaw 600 men but only 396 were actually enlisted and it seems that this levy was the last one among Christians. In fact, we can consider the years 1835–37 as exceptional and corresponding to the clash between Sultan Mahmud II and Mehmed Ali. From now on, the Ottoman navy was to be exclusively Muslim in composition.

Table 4: The Personnel of the Navy in 1845

Categories	Muslims		Christians		Total
	Numbers	Percentage	Numbers	Percentage	
Sailors	7325	91.7	660	8.3	7985
Soldiers	825	100	0	0	825
Danubian	142	100	0	0	142
Arsenal	962	86.3	153	13.7	1115
Workshops	323	46.3	375	53.7	698
Total	9577	89	1188	11	10,765

Excluding officers, who are not included in this table, we get a total of 10,765, with only 7985 real sailors and 1813 workers. Christians were missing in the Marine corps and the Danubian brigade and represented only 8.3 per cent of the sailors.

In the 1830s, the old system of campaign levies was given up for the benefit of a ten year military service, which had already been introduced in the army, based on the drawing of lots for the total number of men to be enlisted each year. Only some of the warships were in commission with their complete crew on board; the others were laid up or under repair with only a restricted complement. In 1846, the situation was as follows.[14] Only five out of twelve ships of the line were in commission, seven out of twenty frigates, and three out of seven corvettes. However, all nine brigantines were in service.

As in the army, the sailors were organized in companies of one hundred men under the command of a *yüzbaşı* and a *mülazim*. The complement of a warship included a number of companies that varied according to its size: for example, a first-rate vessel had eight companies.

Faced with the necessity of finding Muslim seamen, the Ottoman government looked for, and found, new regions for recruitment:

Table 5: Origins of Muslim Sailors (1846–8)

Region	1846		1848	
	Number	Percentage	Number	Percentage
Pontic Anatolia	961	94.7	1864	93.2
Aegean Anatolia	2	0.2	7	0.3
Marmara coasts	24	2.4	79	4.0
Rumelia	19	1.9	50	2.5
Others	8	0.8	0	0
Total	1014	100	2000	100

In 1846–8, not only were almost all the sailors Muslim but they were now recruited almost exclusively in the coastal provinces of Pontic Anatolia, that is to say, the districts of Canik and Trabzon. The old recruiting zones of the Aegean islands, Western Anatolia and even the Marmara area were given up and provided only a very small intake, similar to that of Rumelia.

The officers

Of course, the main question about the 500 men who formed the body of officers was their ability to practice their trade, which consisted of waging war at sea. Selim III's efforts to organize naval and military training did not survive his death. Not until thirty years later, under Mahmud II, was a Naval College created in 1838 in Istanbul. In 1846, it had 180 pupils divided in three classes.

The pupils entered this school individually, and that causes these undated promotions, which are only fixed when several pupils have gained the knowledge necessary to enter this or that service of the navy. It is after the pupils have passed their final exams that they are nominated to serve in the fleet under the name of Mühendis (engineer) and as such assigned to nautical calculations or to the shipway, or under the name of Hodja (clerk) assigned to a function aboard ship such as steering or signals . . . Instruction given to these young men firstly consists of the study of the Turkish, Persian and French languages, then come arithmetic, geometry, algebra, trigonometry and navigation. Bezout, Renaud and Fournier are the authors whose textbooks are read . . . Although this school has been in existence for several years, the number of pupils shared out amongst the different services of the navy is not very high yet and I'll believe the personnel of the navy reorganized only when most of the officers will come from this school instead of the ranks.[15]

In fact, things were running slowly in the navy: in 1849, only two out of a shortlist of sixteen senior officers, were graduates from the Naval College. Nevertheless, the impulse had been given, the spirit of modernization, which had never been lacking in the navy, increased, and the grim memories of Navarino were fading until 30 November 1853. On that day, six Russian first-rate vessels and two frigates under Admiral Nakhimov attacked an Ottoman squadron of six frigates and four corvettes moored in the bay of Sinop and commanded by Admiral Osman Pasha.

The action requires no description. Quite apart from their great superiority in number of guns, the Russians were equipped to fire shell and the Turks were not. In little more then an hour the Turkish squadron had ceased to exist. . . . Osman Pasha and three of his Captains were taken prisoner, while the total loss of the side of the Turks has been put at 3000 or more. That of the Russians was 37 killed and 229 wounded; by no means a negligible number for so one-sided an affair.[16]

Once more, all the efforts spent by the Ottomans to build an efficient and reliable navy seemed reduced to naught, but nothing of the kind. The battle of Sinop was the last which saw sailing warships in action. In the very next years, the combination of steam, armour and shell made all wooden sailing fleets obsolete, in one stroke. Here was a unique opportunity to start the creation of a modern navy from scratch. This opportunity was firmly taken by the Ottoman Empire in the 1860's, confirming its absolute will to remain a great maritime power.

Notes

1 Most of the data are drawn from I. Bostan, *Osmanlı Bahriye Teşkilâti: XVII. Yüzyılda tersane-i-amire* (Ankara, 1992), pp. 181–241. The archives consulted are *Başbakanlık Arşivi, Maliyeden Müdevver Defterler Tasnifi*.

2 İsmail Hakkı Uzunçarşılı, *Osmanlı devletinin merkez ve bahriye teşkilâti* (Ankara, 1948; 3rd edn., 1988), p. 470.

3 R.C. Anderson, *Naval Wars in the Levant 1559–1853* (Liverpool, 1952), pp. 195–7.

4 Uzunçarşılı, *Bahriye*, p. 481.

5 In fact, 801 because the *levend*s were lacking in the list of 1699, although there were 200 during the previous and following years (Bostan, *Osmanlı bahriye*, p. 183).

6 For 1699, see Bostan, *Osmanlı Bahriye*, p. 186; for 1738 see Daniel Panzac, 'La Flotte de guerre ottomane au milieu du XVIIIe siècle', *Belleten* 60 (1996), p. 389–419. [Perhaps the incredibly high number for 1738 should be seen in the light of the existence of ghost sailors similar to the ghost soldiers described in Aksan's article? Ed.]

7 The British navy distinguished thirty-seven specialities among the complement of a vessel in the middle of the eighteenth century; N.A.M. Rodger, *The Wooden World: An Anatomy of the Georgian Navy* (London, 1986), pp. 348–50.

8 For 1693–9, Bostan, *Osmanlı Bahriye*, p. 183; for 1738, Panzac, 'La Flotte de guerre'; for 1815, Uzunçarşılı, *Bahriye Teıkilâti*, pp. 474–5.

9 To counter this danger, the Ottomans asked that French ships be chartered by the Ottomans, a practice called 'caravane maritime', which became official from 1686 onwards for the Ottomans and from 1688 for the French. See Daniel Panzac, *Commerce et navigation dans l'Empire ottoman au XVIIIe siècle* (Istanbul, 1986).

10 *Essay sur la puissance navale des Turcs*, MAE (Foreign Ministry archives), *Mémoires et documents*, vol. 30., fos. 350–51. One example among many it gives: almost all officers and every company of men in charge of a cannon had their own individual stove. That represents several dozen fireplaces and as many risks of setting the vessel alight.

11 'She looked like something in an old print. Without her flag she could have taken her place in the fighting line in Blake's navy or Van [*sic*] Tromp's without exciting comment. She must be almost the last survivor of the small, clumsy ships of the line that had now been replaced by the stately "74"' (C.S. Forrester, *Hornblower and the Atropos* (London, 1990), p. 243.

12 Stanford J. Shaw, 'Selim III and the Ottoman Navy', *Turcica* 1 (1969), pp. 212–41.

13 F. Hitzel, 'Rélations interculturelles et scientifiques entre l'Empire ottoman et les pays de l'Europe occidentale (1453–1839)', unpublished PhD thesis (Paris – Sorbonne IV, 1994).

14 *Statistique de la marine ottomane au 1er juillet 1846*, Service Historique de la Marine, Vincennes, SHM BB 7/6.

15 Ibid.

16 Anderson, *Naval Wars in the Levant*, p. 580.

3· The Nation and its Deserters: Conscription in Mehmed Ali's Egypt

Khaled Fahmy

'Could a Nation, in any true sense of the word, really be born without war?' Such was the question raised by the eminent Oxford military historian Michael Howard in a public lecture on 'War and the Nation-State'.[1] Looking generally at European history in the past two centuries he argued that war was indeed central for the appearance of the modern nation-state and that modern armies are intimately linked to the rise of nationalism. During the first half of the nineteenth century this argument could very well be applied to Egypt. Having been incorporated in the Ottoman Empire for more than two and a half centuries, Egypt, by the beginning the nineteenth century and mostly through an unprecedented war effort that was concurrent and often synonymous with state-building, had come to play an increasingly independent role on the international plane.

Mehmed Ali, who ruled Egypt for the impressively long period of over forty years (1805–48), is the one who is very often praised for affecting this change. His efforts at revitalizing agriculture, reforming the educational system, transforming the legal establishment, and introducing modern industry are often seen as qualifying him for the title of 'Founder of Modern Egypt.'[2] However, it is his founding of a modern army that allows him to occupy this unique position in modern Egyptian historiography. Started in the early 1820s, this army was central to all his reforms: the different schools, factories and hospitals were all founded to serve it, and it was their *raison d'être*. Indeed, such was the close interconnection between the military and other sectors of the state and the economy that Egypt, by the late 1820s and for all practical considerations, had become a military state. Armed to its teeth, Egypt midway in Mehmed Ali's long career had managed to expand its borders and to incorporate neighbouring areas that included the Sudan, Syria, Western Arabia, Yemen, Crete and large parts of southern Anatolia, an achievement that nationalist historians typically bask in.

Above all, though, it is the fact that it was a conscript army that makes this institution occupy a prominent position in Egyptian nationalist historiography. It is often argued that by conscripting the Egyptian peasantry, and by giving them the chance to bear arms and to defend their fatherland for the first time in centuries and even in millennia, this army allowed the soldiers to discover their true identity; that is, that they were essentially and truly Egyptians and that their identities as Muslims or as Ottoman subjects were either artificial or secondary. One modern nationalist historian put it thus: '[The peasants] who for centuries had been tied down to the land and cheated of their liberties, were at last to be resurrected from oblivion and to be taught for the first time since Saladin the fundamental lessons of citizenship and nationalism.'[3] The problem with this argument is that the population of Egypt, as will be shown below, far from enthusiastically flocking to serve in the army, was in fact very resentful of military service and strongly resisted joining the colours. Recognizing that the scale of resistance was alarming, it is still common to argue that this was only a temporary reaction caused above all by 'the fellah's strong attachment to his land and the unfamiliarity of military life to him'.[4] The opposition to service in the 'national' institution is explained away by insisting that this opposition was caused by the 'fellahin's' strong attachment to the land, a sentiment that proves their 'nationalist' feelings. Once the 'fellahin' came to realize the benefits of military life and that serving in the army is the most truthful way of defending their lands they loved so much, they ceased to resist it and ultimately even became proud of belonging to it.[5] The rural population of Egypt was, accordingly, taught that serving in the army, while requiring them to abandon their beloved lands, was in fact the best way to express their loyalty to Egypt and to defend it with their lives if need be, and the Pasha's army was seen as the 'school' in which they were 'taught' how to identify themselves as 'Egyptians'. This identity now appeared as natural and more essential than any local or religious identity they might have adopted. Being a Muslim or an Ottoman subject was suddenly seen as either 'artificial' or secondary compared to this 'primordial' identity. In that sense the army that Mehmed Ali founded is seen as 'the prime pillar of Egyptian independence'.[6]

In this chapter, I take issue with this powerful, monolithic discourse of Egyptian nationalism. I shall question the validity of the claim that the army played a significant role in awakening the Egyptian peasants from their long slumber and in enlightening them as to their true, but hidden, identity. By reviewing the origins of the idea of conscripting the Egyptian peasantry, the initial steps taken to raise men from the countryside, and the reaction that this unprecedented move triggered in the rural population, it is hoped that a truer assessment of the nature of the army can be gleaned. I shall concentrate on the peasants' reaction to what is supposed to be the national institution, and argue that acts of resistance by the peasant-conscripts show not their true and umbilical attachment to their lands, but their aversion to Mehmed Ali's policies and to his officers' elitist practices towards them.

The ethnic composition of the army

Before looking closely at the manner in which the men were conscripted, though, it is important to elaborate on an important feature of the army, namely, the ethnic division between the officers and the men. For when he first conceived of founding a conscript army, Mehmed Ali certainly had no intention of allowing Arabic-speaking Egyptians to assume senior positions in the army. Rather, his plan was to appoint his personal slaves (Mamluks) to high positions, and his Turkish-speaking officers to lower ranks, while the Egyptian conscripts would make up the soldiery.[7] Eventually, Mamluks and 'Turks' fused together into one group and it became difficult to differentiate between them. The main distinction, however, was between soldiers and officers: soldiers were Arabic-speaking, while officers spoke Turkish. For the Pasha clearly had in mind the idea of creating a conscript army in which the soldiers would be firmly dominated by their officers. He once told a distinguished French visitor, 'I have not done in Egypt anything except what the British are doing in India; they have an army composed of Indians and ruled by British officers, and I have an army composed of Arabs ruled by Turkish officers . . . The Turk makes a better officer, since he knows that he is entitled to rule, while the Arab feels that the Turk is better than him in that respect.'[8]

As a rule Arabic-speaking Egyptians, referred to as *evlad-ı Arab*, ('sons of Arabs'), were not allowed to be promoted beyond the rank of captain and very few were promoted to even that rank. As to lieutenants and second lieutenants, half of them had to be 'Turks' and the other half

'Arabs'. Before signing the orders promoting men to these ranks, Ibrahim Pasha, Mehmed Ali's son and commander-in-chief of his forces, inquired if the nominees were from 'those who can be promoted to these ranks, since it is against the rules to have more than four Arab lieutenants per battalion'. Nominations for promotions to upper ranks, on the other hand, usually stated the place of birth of the candidate, to make it clear that he was a 'Turk.'

Being a Turk – that is, speaking Turkish and having one's origins in Anatolia, Istanbul, Albania, or other parts of the Ottoman world – was therefore enough for a man to be considered a candidate for a senior position in Mehmed Ali's army, even if he had originally been captured as a POW![9] After Egypt's defeats of the Ottoman army in the 1831–3 Syrian campaigns, many Ottoman officers and soldiers were taken prisoner. A number of them were appointed officers in the Egyptian army in Syria, a policy that caused much resentment among the soldiers. They complained saying, 'Why do we sacrifice our lives and put ourselves in danger to capture these men only to find them appointed as our officers ruling above us?'[10] Neither Mehmed Ali nor Ibrahim found any problems with this practice, although Ibrahim, being closer to the soldiers and more sensitive to their sentiments, might have been more apprehensive than his father about it. As far as both men were concerned, these were *evlad-ı Türk* ('sons of Turks'), who were more entitled and capable than 'Arabs' to be appointed officers.

These basic and essential differences between officers and soldiers caused considerable tension between the two groups. Some officers cheated their soldiers, selling them goods at ten times the market price, 'until they were left penniless'. The habit of insulting and abusing soldiers was so widespread that Ibrahim had to write and distribute a general pamphlet to all the regiments in Syria, reminding the officers that it was due primarily to the 'bravery and zeal' of the soldiers that the army was victorious in its numerous battles. He ordered them not to abuse or insult their soldiers, and to send them to a court martial (*divan*) to be tried there according to the law, rather than take the law in their own hands. He warned the officers that anyone found violating these orders would be expelled from the service.[11]

In spite of this clear and stern warning, however, it proved difficult to force the officers to treat the soldiers respectfully and complaints about such bad treatment did not stop. Even if one argues that Ibrahim was more sensitive than his father concerning the sentiments of his 'Arab' soldiers, the problems he had with his officers were deeply ingrained in the army and were much too formidable to be solved by his ostensibly liberal ideas.[12] In other words, when push came to shove Ibrahim knew were his true interests lay: with his father and the Mamluk–Turkish elite that formed the core of the officer corps.

If the ethnic composition of the army betrays its dynastic as opposed to its alleged national character, can it be argued that the soldiers, nevertheless, saw the army as a national army, one that was fighting for the defence or the glory of the fatherland? Having seen that the ethnic division between them and their officers was an inbuilt feature of the army they served in, can one still present an argument that within that particular institution the soldiers had the opportunity to participate in an experience that would make them think of themselves as 'Egyptians'? Could it be said that the army, although not intended to create such feeling, might have created it unwittingly?

To answer these questions, we shall have to follow the soldiers closely after conscription. Conscription and the peasants' reaction to it are the litmus test that can detect the nature of the army and check the allegation that it was in fact a national one.

Origins of the idea of a regular standing army

When Mehmed Ali became governor of Egypt in 1805 at the young age of thirty-five, he was aware that he had been given one of the wealthiest Ottoman provinces to rule. However, he was not deceived into thinking that his position was a secure one. For one thing, he came to power as a result of a 'revolutionary moment' in Cairo, whereby a coalition of local forces had coerced the remote Ottoman government to submit to their demands and to appoint Mehmed Ali against its wishes. The Pasha therefore knew only too well that his appointment, while decreed by Istanbul, had in fact been forced on Sultan Selim, and he was wary that he might be deposed at the earliest opportunity. This wariness haunted Mehmed Ali throughout his long career as governor of Egypt, and Egypt's history in the first half of the nineteenth century was considerably shaped by his attempt to make his tenure more secure and permanent.

Crucially, he lacked a reliable military force that would entrench him more firmly in his prized province and which would enable him to confront any attempt by the Sultan to dislodge him. With this aim in mind he went ahead with characteristic methodical thoroughness, first disposing of the Mamluk chieftains in the infamous massacre of the

Citadel in 1811, then four years later (in 1815) unsuccessfully attempting to subdue the rebellious Albanian contingent that had brought him
to power ten years earlier, and finally in 1820 launching a daring but
disastrous campaign to the Sudan to collect men for his planned army.
After four years in the Sudan his Turkish-speaking forces had managed
to gather 20,000 men, but only 3000 were still alive; the others had
perished 'like sheep with the rot'.[13]

It was this last attempt that prompted Mehmed Ali to turn finally to
the population of Egypt to supply him with the desperately needed
manpower for his army. Conscripting the Egyptians was resorted to not
because they were believed to make good soldiers, let alone because they
were thought to be entitled to serve in their country's army, but because
Mehmed Ali could not satisfy his dynastic needs by using any other
source of manpower. The fateful decision to conscript the Egyptian
peasants was specifically triggered by Mehmed Ali's desire to protect his
fellow 'Turks': when he realized that the Sudan campaign was turning
into a fiasco, and especially when he was informed that a large number
of his Turkish-speaking officers were deserting and returning *en masse*
to Egypt, he wrote to the governor of one of the southern provinces telling him that, 'since the Turks are members of our race and since they
must be spared the trouble of being sent to remote and dangerous areas,
it has become necessary to conscript around 4,000 men from Upper
Egypt [to replace them]'. These troops, he went on to explain, were to
be drafted for a period of three years after which they would be given a
stamped certificate and allowed to return to their villages.[14] Dated early
1822, this was the first conscription order issued by the Pasha in Cairo,
and it ushered in a long and burdensome policy that exhausted the
Egyptian countryside in an unprecedented manner.

The new conscripts were sent to training camps in Upper Egypt
where the nucleus of the officer corps was also being formed from
Mamluks belonging to the Pasha and to members of his family, mainly
his son Ibrahim Pasha. While the new soldiers were being drilled, the
officers were also being trained by a group of French officers who had
earlier served in Napoleon's army and who were seeking employment
after the demobilization of the Emperor's military forces. Chief among
them was a certain officer by the name of Sèves, who claimed to have
been a colonel in Napoleon's army and to have witnessed Waterloo and
whom the French Consul-General in Egypt, Bernardino Drovetti, had
introduced to the Pasha. Sèves eventually converted to Islam, took the
Muslim name of Suleyman Agha, and rose in the military hierarchy to

acquire the title of Pasha and to be second only to Ibrahim Pasha, the Pasha's son and commander-in-chief of his forces. The Ottoman model was not far from the Pasha's eyes, however, when he planned his new army. For soon after commanding Sèves to attend to his business, he explicitly ordered Ibrahim Pasha to adopt the structure that Sultan Selim III had used in his own army more than twenty years earlier. 'Although the plan that Suleyman Agha has put forward is a wonderful one,' he told Ibrahim, 'it is similar to the one that Napoleon had used to lead an army composed of several thousand troops. Our army, however, is a new and much smaller one and we have only recently begun to create it.'[15]

Both Mehmed Ali and Ibrahim had practical minds and they had no difficulty adopting the Ottoman model to fit their new army while at the same time borrowing from the French the idea of conscripting and arming the peasants. Unlike the French army, however, Mehmed Ali's new army, as was said above, was to be ethnically divided. This division had two aims. First, it was intended to be a means of attracting men from all over the Ottoman world to come and serve Mehmed Ali and his expanding household. Through these positions and others in the civilian bureaucracy, which was also rapidly expanding, a loyal elite was being cemented around the Pasha and his family. Second, it aimed to deny the Arabic-speaking masses the possibility of challenging the Pasha's rule if they assumed leadership roles.

The need to keep the peasants, the overwhelming majority of the Arabic-speaking masses, in this inferior and submissive position was felt to be especially crucial, for in addition to the potential danger to agricultural production that moving these thousands of men would cause, conscripting the peasantry was an unprecedented move whose danger lay in giving them arms precisely at a time when resentment of the government's harsh policies was already high. By the 1820s the Pasha had instituted a wide-ranging monopolies programme and had extended it to include most major staple foodstuffs and many other cash crops. In addition, and in order to undertake his numerous and often ambitious public works programmes, the Pasha had much wider recourse to corvée than had previously been seen in Egypt. As if this was not enough, to finance his various projects the Pasha had increased land tax so much that by the 1820s the countryside had reached the limit of its ability to meet his insatiable needs.[16]

As a result of this deeply felt resentment of the Pasha and his policies, the countryside could not withstand yet more pressure put on it. The decision to conscript the fallahin had serious repercussions which posed an alarming threat to Mehmed Ali's authority. In 1823, immediately after conscription was introduced in Lower Egypt, a big revolt erupted in Minufiyya province and the Pasha had to go there in person guarded by his own palace troops and assisted by six field-cannon to subdue the revolt. The following year an even larger rebellion broke out in Upper Egypt and was soon joined by more than 30,000 men and women. Looting, arson and attacks on local officials were reported to the Pasha, who decided to deal with the rebellion by sending his newly formed troops to quell the revolt.

This was a serious gamble, for the troops were sent to the very provinces from which they themselves had been conscripted. The risk paid off, though, when one of the new regiments marched into the centre of the revolt in Qina, and managed to quell the revolt in only two weeks, leaving 4000 casualties. The new troops had two other chances to prove themselves. A contingent of 2500 troops that had been sent to the Hijaz to deal with renewed fighting in Arabia inflicted a decisive defeat on a force of Wahabi warriors ten times its size. A short while later, on 24 March 1824, a huge explosion took place in a powder magazine inside the Citadel in Cairo and more than 4000 people were killed. There were rumours that the explosion was the work of the old Albanian troops, who had been hard hit by the Pasha's creation of his new disciplined troops. This posed a grave danger to the Pasha, whose position was compared to that of Sultan Selim when he unsuccessfully attempted to get rid of his old-guard Janissary troops seventeen years earlier. A single battalion of the new troops, however, rushed to the scene, isolated the powder magazine, and quickly brought the situation under control.

These repeated tests that the new troops passed fascinated Mehmed Ali and he set his bureaucratic machinery going to conscript more and more peasants into his new army. Starting with a mere 4000 men, the number of conscripts reached the impressive figure of 130,000 troops less than ten years later. While the army's significance does not lie solely in its size, understanding the manner in which this large number of men was conscripted is central to knowing the nature of the government machinery behind it, as well as its impact on the rural population of Egypt.[17]

Conscription methods

As noted above, the first attempt at conscripting the Egyptian fellahin stemmed from the desire to relieve the Turkish soldiers in Mehmed

Ali's pay from serving in the remote and hot lands of the Sudan. The 4000 peasants gathered from villages in Upper Egypt to replace them were to be conscripted for only three years, at the end of which they would each be given a stamped certificate and allowed to return to their villages and resume their normal, civilian lives. They were to be collected not by the village sheikh but by an officer sent from Cairo for that purpose. The sheikh was only to assist him in finding men in his village who were suitable for military service.[18]

When issuing the conscripting officers their orders, Mehmed Ali tried to impress upon them that they had to handle this important task delicately. He wrote to Ibrahim Pasha telling him that he had been informed that the conscripting officers were gathering men from the villages in the same manner as collecting men for corvée. He told him that this method must be stopped at once:

Since the fellahin are not used to military service, they should not be dragged into the army by force. We have to attract their minds to it . . . This can be done by employing some preachers who should convince the fellahin that [serving in the army] is not like corvée. . . Alternatively, we can remind them of how easy it was for the French [while they were in Egypt] to collect Copts to serve in their army due to their eagerness to serve their faith. If that was the case with the Copts, it will certainly be more so with the fellahin, whose hearts have been inflamed by their religiosity and their zeal in defending Islam.[19]

This was wishful thinking on the part of the Pasha. In fulfilling their duties, the conscripting officers encountered problems that were much too serious to be solved by simply appointing preachers to attract the minds of the fellahin to military service. Besides lacking any detailed information about the population, the authorities did not yet have a reliable medical system to screen the conscripts. Moreover, unlike the recruiting officers of the French Revolutionary and Napoleonic armies,[20] for example, the officers sent from Cairo to conscript the fellahin had no guidelines with regard to the age, marital status or number of brothers of the men they should conscript. Lacking this vital information, the officers, on receiving their orders, would descend upon any given village and seize as many men as they could find, 'without any order, arrangement, inscription, or lot-drawing'.[21] The men were then tied together with ropes round their necks in groups of six or eight,[22] and marched off to the training camps, escorted by the conscription gang. They left behind a 'heart-stricken, sorrowful group' of wives, mothers and children wailing and screaming and hopelessly trying to prevent the soldiers from taking away their men.[23]

All attempts to persuade the fellahin that serving in the army was a religious duty and that being drafted was not like corvée labour fell on deaf ears. Even before the Pasha had turned against the Ottoman Sultan, the call to arms in defence of the faith, either against the Greek 'rebels' or the Wahabis of Arabia, who were seen as 'heretics', was a completely alien and meaningless call with little or no emotional appeal. 'A recruiting party with all the allurements of drums, ribbons, and promises, might march from Rosetta to Assouan without picking up a single volunteer'.[24] Anxious about their families and about their land, which would necessarily lie fallow, the peasants found little incentive to join the colours, and, given the illogical, arbitrary and unsparing method of conscription, they attempted to resist it through all means possible.

Reaction to conscription

Here we come to the nub of the problem facing Mehmed Ali and his military authorities: the Pasha never succeeded in inducing the fellahin to join the colours of their free will by employing ideological or religious arguments. Soon after the new policy became known in the countryside, the fellahin employed different methods to escape the conscription gangs. One method was open rebellion, and mention has already been made of the two rebellions that broke out in 1823–34 as a result of introducing conscription on a large scale. Besides rebelling, the fellahin often deserted their villages altogether to avoid being taken into the army. As soon as news of the approach of a recruiting party reached a village – 'and it spread over the country like wildfire'[25] – a wave of desertions followed, with masses of families fleeing their homes and villages in desperate attempts to evade conscription. By the late 1830s this practice was so widespread that entire villages were found abandoned: 'buried in their stillness, . . . where the dwellings of the poor inhabitants . . . still standing, neither blackened by fire, nor destroyed by war, nor decayed by time, but deprived of their inhabitants [who attempted to avoid the agents of the Pasha] by giving up house and home, and deserting, *en masse*, the beloved town or village'.[26]

When the fellahin saw that open revolt and group desertion were ineffective ways of evading the conscription gangs, they resorted to more tragic means of rebellion. One method was to maim themselves so as to be declared medically unfit for service. Initially, the most common mutilation was removal of their front teeth so as to be deemed incapable of tearing open the paper cartridges when loading a musket. However, when Mehmed Ali was informed that a lot of men in Upper Egypt had resorted to this habit, he said that, since the training manuals did not specify which teeth should be used in loading the musket, these men could use other teeth and should therefore still be conscripted.[27] Other ways of maiming were more dangerous and resulted in serious bodily harm. For example, some fellahin resorted to blinding themselves (or at least causing serious inflammation) by putting rat poison in their eyes. On hearing about this terrible practice, Mehmed Ali wrote to his provincial governors forbidding the spice merchants to sell rat poison. As for those unfortunates who had actually used it, they were sentenced to life imprisonment in the infamous prison of Alexandria, the *liman* of Abu Qir.[28] In one case a woman gouged out the eyes of two men, one a soldier who had deserted from the army, and the other her son (who might have been asked to join the army himself). On being informed about this case, the Pasha ordered her to be drowned in the Nile; the deserter was sent to the liman of Abu Qir, and her son was pardoned.[29] When these practices became 'very common'[30] the Pasha resolved to punish the mutilated men and their accomplices severely by sending them to prison for life, as well as conscripting their relatives instead of them;[31] and to deter those who assisted the men in maiming themselves, usually their wives or mothers, an order was issued to hang these women at the entrances of their villages so 'as to be an example to others'.[32] If the maimed were of no practical use to the army, they were sent to the *liman* of Alexandria for life.[33] Otherwise, if it was judged that they would be useful in other government establishments, they were sent there. For example, when workers were demanded for the a new powder-magazine, Mehmed Ali ordered 120 of those who had maimed themselves, either by gouging out an eye or by chopping off a finger, to be sent to work in his new establishment.[34]

A clear message was being delivered to the Pasha and his military authorities: the peasants resented his army and were going to extreme lengths to resist serving in it. In response, the Pasha was sending back an equally clear message to anyone who might be thinking of mutilating himself to evade conscription: he would still be taken for the service, if not for the army, for another of the Pasha's projects. In short, it proved extremely difficult to evade conscription, for it seems that the Pasha was stubbornly determined that the mutilated would not be spared. When all methods failed to deter the peasants from following this terrible practice, the authorities went ahead with drafting the maimed all the same. On visiting Asyut in 1834, a British traveller described 'a whole regiment which had been composed of mutilated conscripts, every one of whom had either lost an eye, a finger, or the front teeth'.[35]

Desertion

Alarming as these cases are, they still do not reveal the degree of aversion that the peasants felt towards Mehmed Ali's army, an aversion that can best be seen when the scale, nature, and frequency of desertion are studied closely. For the soldiers fighting in Mehmed Ali's army deserted at the slightest opportunity. They fled from the camps and during marches. They escaped from military hospitals, from military ships, from military schools, and from military establishments. Not only soldiers but NCOs fled. More significantly, the guards themselves fled and even in the elite regiments, the Guardia regiments, created to catch deserters, among other things, desertion was rampant.

Desertion was not a matter of individual isolated cases that the authorities succeeded in limiting and controlling; it was so common and on such a large scale that the regiments' scribes were given pre-printed tables with '*Noksan*', ('missing'), as one of the standard headings.[36] Both Mehmed Ali and his son were alarmed at the scale of the problem. Ibrahim rejected the officers' claim that it was the soldiers' increased duties that prompted them to desert. He said that this was a mere pretext and that desertion was more due to the laxity and carelessness of the officers.[37] His father was of a similar opinion. He wrote to the director of his War Department telling him that he had seen reports of the various regiments and, with only one exception, desertion was rife in them all. The exception was the Eighteenth Infantry Regiment, which he took to be proof that desertion could be prevented. He therefore suggested that the colonels of the other regiments be court-martialled.[38]

Having succeeded in escaping from their units, where did the men go? One obvious destination was their villages. After a check of the registers to identify the deserters' villages, however, an order would be issued to the governor of the province in which the villages lay.[39] The order gave the deserters' names and descriptions, and when they were found the head of the village (*sheikh al-balad*) was fined fifty piastres for each one, as well as receiving 100 strokes of the whip.[40] Spies (*bassassin*) were also sent roaming the countryside searching for deserters.[41]

Otherwise, deserters left for Cairo in the hope that they would not be found, since it was supposedly more difficult to spot strangers there.[42] To curb this, the director of the War Department ordered quarter and street sheikhs to keep an eye open for all deserters who might have sought refuge in the city.[43] This was also one of the important functions of the Cairo police (*Zabtiyyat Misr*).[44]

Finding it difficult to go back to their villages or to disappear in the anonymity of Cairo, some soldiers attempted to leave Egypt altogether, although even that proved difficult since the Bedouin were always on the lookout for deserters.[45] In spite of this strict surveillance, however, some soldiers managed to escape to the Hijaz and the Pasha had to write to his nephew, Ahmed Pasha Yeğen, who was military governor there, to catch all deserters who sought refuge there.[46] When it was discovered that some soldiers were posing as pilgrims in order to escape to Arabia,[47] all pilgrims were ordered to have a stamped certificate stating their names, the names of their villages and their physical descriptions.[48] Finally, when one of the Egyptian officials that the Pasha had sent to France told the Pasha that he had found a number of deserters in Paris (!), Mehmed Ali in desperation and frustration admitted that desertion was impossible to stop, but that did not mean that nothing could be done about it and he urged senior officers to discuss ways of limiting desertion from their regiments.[49]

Besides ordering the sheikhs to capture any deserters who might have taken refuge in their villages, and telling them they would be whipped if they did not comply,[50] Mehmed Ali threatened his own officers 'for any negligence that [they] showed in that respect'. Any officer from whose unit a deserter fled had to find a replacement himself. If he failed to do so, a percentage of his salary would be deducted.[51] Furthermore, it was decreed that deserters who had decided voluntarily to return to their units would be pardoned; otherwise on being caught they would each receive 500 strokes of the whip.[52] In another desperate attempt to control desertion people who caught deserters were rewarded with fifty piastres for each one they caught.[53] Yet the Pasha knew quite well that responsibility for catching deserters ultimately rested with local and provincial officials; he warned them that, if they were not strict in that respect, he would forget their previous services and would beat them up himself.[54]

In spite of all these orders and decrees, in spite of the heavy surveillance that they were under, and in spite of the drastic punishments inflicted upon those who were caught, the peasants were deserting in a steady stream and nothing that the authorities did was effective enough in stopping them from doing so. During the early years of the Syrian campaigns (1831–3) it was difficult to know exactly how many men went missing from their units at any one time; the roll-calls gave estimates as low as 10 per cent and as high as 25 per cent of any one regiment.[55] Fifteen years after the introduction of conscription, however, Mehmed Ali received a report which was most alarming regarding deserters. It said that as many as 60,000 men had gone missing from the army, in addition to 20,000 from the navy![56] Bearing in mind that the army could not have been larger than 130,000, this means that for every three conscripts, one soldier managed to desert.

One of the main reasons why conscription was hated so much was that it was for an unlimited period, in spite of the Pasha's initial order to have it limited to three years. When Ibrahim Pasha realized this after more than ten years of active conscription, in which time the countryside had been drained of its male population, he wrote to his father suggesting that service should be for a fixed period. He explained:

> It is natural for any sane person to resist conscription, since [they view] conscription and captivity as one and the same thing. No conscript would ever have the hope of saying, 'I will be conscripted for a fixed period, then I will be discharged and live the remaining years of my life [with my family].' Men have the right to think like this, since we do not discharge them unless they receive serious wounds in their hands, legs, eyes or heads; that is, they are discharged only if they are good neither for the army nor [for any other] service. This is why we face resistance in conscripting the peasants.[57]

After thinking about it, Mehmed Ali saw the logic of his son's suggestion and wrote back telling him that he had decided to limit the period – to fifteen years! Ibrahim said he was going to announce the good news to the soldiers, thinking that this showed how merciful and benevolent the Benefactor, as Mehmed Ali was commonly known in Egypt, was.[58] On second thoughts, however, his father said that this way they would lose a lot of men and suggested that the new system be applied only to the new conscripts and that those already in service should be treated as if they had spent only five years already; that is, they would be kept for another ten years.[59]

Given this mentality, it was natural for the male population of Egypt to hate the army into which they were dragged by Mehmed Ali's war machine and to seize every opportunity to evade it whenever and wherever possible. Nothing could be further from the truth than the common allegation by nationalist historians that the Egyptian peasants eventually saw that 'military life was more comfortable than their village life [which, in fact, is not saying much], and even became proud of it'.[60] In all the numerous cases about conscripting the male population of Egypt into Mehmed Ali's army there was only a single case about a man joining the army voluntarily. He had been released and allowed to go back to his village, then some time later came back saying that he had heard from some pilgrims that his village had been deserted and that none of his relatives or friends had remained behind.[61] This could hardly be viewed as a positive reason for joining the army Mehmed Ali founded, the 'prime pillar of Egyptian independence'.

The frequency and scale of desertion are more eloquent than any allegations by nationalist historians regarding how the population of Egypt thought of the Pasha's army and his regime in general. Desertion was the most striking testimony of the fellahin's willingness to resist a regime they found oppressive, intolerant and inhuman. There is something almost splendid about defying Mehmed Ali and his authorities in that way and at that level. Desertion and the authorities' frustration with it show that Mehmed Ali's policies had no echo in the peasants' minds and hearts. The Pasha might have created an elaborate machinery to conscript and train the peasants. He managed to aggregate their forces and organize them along European lines and to fight his wars with them successfully. But just as he managed to create what appeared to be a disciplined soldiery, the peasants, through desertion, asserted their power to disrupt his machinery and to contest his wish to subjugate them.

When studying the army of Egypt in the first half of the nineteenth century, an army that is supposed to have been the national institution *par excellence*, I found no evidence that this central institution functioned along national lines. To the fellah-soldiers, the allegation that this was their army, fighting for their own sake, would have been the most ludicrous claim they had ever heard. For them, nothing could have been further from the truth. The soldiers came to see the army as the most detestable aspect of the Pasha's already hated regime. They were forced to serve in it for practically their entire lives, often never seeing their families again. During their lifelong period of conscription they were ridiculed, beaten and humiliated by their Turkish-speaking officers. They saw the army as an institution that embodied in the most concrete and direct way the atrocious, inhuman and dreadful policies of Mehmed Ali. Seeing it in this light, they spared no means at their disposal to express their true sentiments of disgust and hatred of the regime that made them pay with their blood and lives for the glory of Mehmed Ali and his family. They may have left us no written records to let us know their feelings towards the army and the Pasha, but they made their thoughts known by much more eloquent means. Through desertion and self-mutilation they showed that they would use any means at all to evade an institution that came to represent to them in a very real way all the brutalities of the Pasha's regime.

Notes

1   Michael Howard, *War and the Nation State* (Oxford, 1978), p. 9. On the connections between armies and the formation of modern nation-states, see Charles Tilly, *Coercion, Capital and European States, AD 990–1990* (Cambridge, MA, 1990), and Anthony Giddens, *The Nation-State and Violence* (Berkeley and Los Angeles, 1985).

2   Henry Herbert Dodwell, *The Founder of Modern Egypt; A Study of Muhammed Ali* (Cambridge, 1931).

3   M.A. Rifa't, *The Awakening of Modern Egypt* (London, 1947), p. 38.

4   Jamil 'Ubaid, *Qissat Ihtilal Muhammad 'Ali lil-Yunan* [The Story of Mehmed Ali's Occupation of Greece] (Cairo, 1990), pp. 79–80; Ahmad 'Izzat 'Abdel-Karim, *Tarikh al-Ta'lim fi 'Asr Muhammad 'Ali* [History of Education in Mehmed Ali's Reign] (Cairo, 1938), pp. 36–7.

5   'Abdel-Rahman al-Raf'i, *'Asr Muhammad 'Ali* [Mehmet Ali's Reign] (Cairo, 1951), p. 331.

6   Ibid, p. 321.

7   Dar al-Watha'iq al-Qawmiyya (Egyptian National Archives; hereafter: DWQ): S/1/48/1/3, on 13 Shawwal 1238 (23 June 1823).

8   Georges Douin, ed., *La Mission du Baron de Boislecomte: L'Egypte et la Syrie en 1833* (Cairo, 1927), pp. 110–11.

9   For the same prerequisites for joining the civil service, see Hilmi A. Shalabi, *al-Muwazzaffun fi Misr fi 'Asr Muhammad 'Ali* [Public Employees in Egypt during the Reign of Mehmed Ali] (Cairo, 1989), pp. 29, 63.

10 DWQ: Sham 11/105, on 12 Rabi' II 1248 (8 September 1832).

11 DWQ: Sham 15/146, on 23 Rajab 1248 (17 December 1832).

12 Ibrahim is quoted by a French military adviser as saying, 'I am not a Turk. I came as a mere child to Egypt, and since then the Egyptian sun has changed my blood and made me wholly Arab.' Douin, *Boislecomte*, p. 249.

For the differences between father and son regarding how to treat the 'Egyptians', see Afaf Lutfi al-Sayyid Marsot, *Egypt in the Reign of Muhammad Ali* (Cambridge, 1984), p. 97.

13 Dodwell, *The Founder of Modern Egypt*, pp. 64–5.

14 DWQ: S/1/50/2/145, on 25 Jumadi I 1237 (18 February 1822).

15 DWQ: S/1/50/2/209, on 18 Rajab 1237 (11 April 1822).

16 Kenneth M. Cuno, *The Pasha's Peasants: Land, Society, and Economy in Lower Egypt, 1740–1858* (Cambridge, 1992), p. 117.

17 For a fuller analysis of the impact of the army on Egyptian society, see Khaled Fahmy, *All the Pasha's Men: Mehmed Ali, His Army and the Making of Modern Egypt* (Cambridge, 1997).

18 DWQ: S/1/50/2/145, on 25 Jumadi I 1237 (18 February 1822).

19 DWQ: S/1/50/2/186, on 6 Rajab 1237 (29 March 1822).

20 Isser Woloch, 'Napoleonic Conscription: State Power and Civil Society', *Past and Present* 111 (1986), pp.102–5; and Alan Forrest, *Conscripts and Deserters: The Army and French Society During the Revolution and Empire* (Oxford, 1989), p. 27.

21 Sir John Bowring, 'Report on Egypt and Candia', *Parliamentary Papers, Reports from Commissioners* 21 (1840), p. 52.

22 Jules Planat, *Histoire de la régénération de l'Egypte* (Paris, 1830), pp. 76–7.

23 James Augustus St John, *Egypt and Mohammed-Ali* (London, 1834), vol. 2, p. 277. See also P.N. Hamont, *L'Egypte sous Méhémet-Ali* (Paris, 1843), vol. 2, p. 12.

24 C. Rochfort Scott, *Rambles in Egypt and Candia* (London, 1837), vol. 2, p. 219.

25 St John, *Egypt and Mohammed-Ali*, vol. 1, p. 189.

26 Richard R. Madden, *Egypt and Mohammed Ali* (London, 1841), pp. 41–2.

27 DWQ: S/1/48/4/648, on 18 Jumadi II 1250 (23 October 1834).

28 Amin Sami, *Taqwim al-Nil* [Chronicle of the Nile] (Cairo, 1928), vol. 2, p. 362, letter dated 17 Sha'ban 1245 (11 January 1830). The *liman* of Alexandria, built in 1829 as the Arsenal Works, eventually became a large prison reserved for serious 'criminals' from all over Egypt and incarcerating them usually for life.

29 Ibid, p. 365: letter dated 13 Dhu al-Qi'da 1245 (6 May 1830). See also the case of the mother who chopped off the finger of her son who had been released from one of the Pasha's schools but was to be taken there again. She was given 200 lashes; S/6/2/1/5, p. 52, on 7 Shawwal 1264 (6 September 1848).

30 Bowring, 'Report on Egypt', p. 52.

31 St John, *Egypt and Mohammed-Ali*, vol. 1, pp. 189–91. See also Scott, *Rambles in Egypt*, vol. 2, pp. 217–18.

32 DWQ: S/1/48/3/235, on 7 Rajab 1243 (25 January 1828).

33 DWQ: S/1/48/4/365, on 14 Shawwal 1249 (23 February 1834); Awamir lil-Jihadiyya 1/159, on 11 Ramadan 1253 (10 December 1837).

34 DWQ: Awamir lil-Jihadiyya 1/150, on 5 Ramadan 1253 (4 December 1837).

35 St John, *Egypt and Mohammed-Ali*, vol. 2, p. 175; see also Bowring, 'Report on Egypt', p. 52.

36 See, for example, DWQ: Sham 10/129, on 16 Rabi' I 1248 (13 August 1832). In this case 128 men out of a battalion of 521 were 'missing'.

37 DWQ: Sham 10/63, on 9 Rabi' I 1248 (6 August 1832).

38 DWQ: Awamir lil-Jihadiyya 1/35, on 27 Muharram 1248 (26 June 1832).

39 Helen Anne B. Rivlin, *The Agricultural Policy of Muhammad 'Ali in Egypt* (Cambridge, MA, 1961), pp. 90–91.

40 DWQ: Dhawat 5/113, on 3 Rabi' I 1246 (22 August 1830).

41 DWQ: S/1/48/4/549, on 2 Rajab 1250 (4 November 1834).

42 DWQ: S/1/48/1/343, on 4 Dhu al-Qi'da 1239 (1 July 1824); Sham 2/71, on 17 Rajab 1247 (22 December 1831).

43 DWQ: Diwan Khedewi 2/273, on 17 Jumadi I 1250 (21 September 1834).

44 DWQ: See, for example, L/2/1/1/14, on 21 Dhu al-Qi'da 1260 (3 December 1844).

45 DWQ: S/1/48/1/331, on 22 Shawwal 1239 (21 June 1824).

46 DWQ: S/1/48/4/92, on 6 Rajab 1249 (19 November 1833).

47 DWQ: S/1/50/5/130, on 14 Jumadi I 1239 (18 November 1823).

48 DWQ: S/1/47/8/353, on 28 Jumadi II 1241 (7 February 1826).

49 DWQ: Dhawat 5/208, on 27 Muharram 1251 (26 May 1835). Neither the nature nor the purpose of the official's visit is stated. His name is given as Mehmed Emin Efendi.

50 DWQ: S/1/47/14/442, on 2 Sha'ban 1244 (7 February 1829).

51 That was for officers from colonel to captain; officers from captain to corporal were beaten: DWQ: Awamir lil-Jihadiyya 1/36, on 28 Muharram 1248 (27 June 1832). For an Arabic translation, see Sami, *Taqwim al-Nil*, vol. 2, pp. 397–8.

52 DWQ: Sham 11/171, on 18 Rabi' II 1248 (14 September 1832). Four deserters who were caught were punished in that way: Sham 11/210, on 21 Rabi' II, 1248 (17 September 1832).

53 DWQ: Sham 2/71, on 15 Rajab 1247 (20 December 1831).

54 DWQ: S/1/47/8/351, on 26 Jumadi II 1241 (6 February 1826).

55 This is based on information from the *yevmiyyet*, the regimental journals. See, for instance, that of the 13th Infantry Regiment in which more than 25 per cent of the soldiers were reported to be missing: DWQ: Sham 23/70, on 1 Muharram, 1249 (21 May 1833); and that of the 12th Infantry Regiment in which 13 per cent were missing: Sham 10/69, on 9 Rabi' II 1248 (6 August 1832).

56 DWQ: Ma'iyya Saniyya, Mulakhkhasat Awamir Mustakhraja min al-
    Dafatir, Box 3, Booklet 28, Order dated 8 Muharram 1253 (14 April 1837).
57 DWQ: Sham 30/510, on 25 Dhu al-Hijja 1250 (25 April 1835).
58 DWQ: Sham 31/6, on 7 Muharram 1251 (5 May 1835).
59 DWQ: Sham 31/62, on 28 Muharram 1251 (27 May 1835).
60 al-Rafi'i, *'Asr Muhammad 'Ali*, p. 331.
61 DWQ: S/1/48/4/407, on 3 Dhu al-Qi'da 1249 (4 March 1834).

4· The Ottoman Conscription System in Theory and Practice, 1844–1918

Erik Jan Zürcher

The introduction of conscription in the Ottoman Empire was of course closely linked to the introduction of a European-style army, but it did not coincide with it.

As is well known, the first attempt to create an army which was trained, equipped and dressed in the contemporary European fashion was made by Sultan Selim III in 1792. His *Nizam-i Cedid* (New Order) army was by all accounts quite an impressive achievement in itself. From an initial strength of about 2500, by 1806 the corps had grown to 22,685 men and 1590 officers, half of them stationed in the capital, the rest in provincial centres in Anatolia. When pressure against him and his new army on the part of the old army establishment, primarily the Janissaries, mounted, however, the sultan succumbed without any attempt to use the considerable strength of his new army and disbanded the corps in 1808.[1]

The *Nizam* troops constituted a professional army. They were not recruited on the basis of universal conscription, but rather in a fashion reminiscent of the system introduced by Peter the Great in Russia or the *bunichah* system in Persia.[2] Governors and notables in Anatolia (not in the Balkans or the Arab provinces) were required to send contingents of peasant boys to Istanbul for training. Those enrolled in the corps remained under arms for an unspecified period.

The reforming Sultan Selim was toppled in 1808, but the arguments for a wide-ranging reform of the army remained as compelling after his demise as they had been before. The great defeats of the Ottoman army by the Russians in 1774 and 1792 had shown up its weakness; the Napoleonic wars and especially the actions of the French and British troops in Egypt and Syria in 1798–1800 had made a deep impression on those who witnessed them; and, from the 1820s onwards, the successes of the pasha of Egypt, Mehmed Ali, with his French-trained army served as a source of both inspiration and envy.[3]

When Mahmud II finally felt secure enough to take up the military reforms of Selim III in 1826, he first tried to avoid the clash with the army establishment which had been fatal to Selim, by forming his modernized army from within the active parts of the Janissaries (most of whom by this time were not soldiers at all, but shopkeepers who held a Janissary pay ticket and thus enjoyed the privileges of the military ruling class). When this, too, met with stiff opposition and even open rebellion, Mahmud had the Janissaries shot to pieces in their barracks. The next day the venerable corps was formally disbanded (although in some provinces Janissary troops continued to exist into the 1840s) and the forming of a new army, the *Muallem Asakir-i Mansure-i Muhammadiye* ('Trained Victorious Muhammadan Soldiers'), was announced.

The new army, which was modelled closely on the earlier *Nizam-i Cedid* corps, quickly grew from 1500 to 27,000 men. It was organized along European lines, the basic unit being the regiment (*tertip*, later *alay*), consisting of three battalions (*tabur*). Once again, this was a professional army manned by volunteers and peasants recruited by the Sultan's officials in the provinces. There was no real system of recruitment, but the ranks of the army were filled according to need. Each year the army's requirements were determined in a decision (*kararname*) of the imperial council and then communicated to the provincial authorities, who were left a free hand in the way they filled their quotas.

Recruitment age was between fifteen and thirty years and the minimum term of service was twelve years. After twelve years the soldiers could opt for a civilian life, but in order to qualify for a pension they were obliged to serve until overtaken by old age or infirmity.

Parallel to the *Mansure* army, a second modernized unit was formed out of the old corps of Imperial Gardeners (*Bostancıyan*), who for centuries had guarded the imperial palaces and the seafront along the Bosphorus. They were now reconstituted as an imperial guard, called the *Hassa* (Special) army, whose strength reached about 11,000 by the end of the 1830s.[4]

In July 1834, a further momentous step in the modernization of the army was the establishment of a reserve army or militia, based on the Prussian *Landwehr*, called the *Asakir-i redife-i mansure* (Victorious Reserve Soldiers), or *Redif* for short. In each province between ten and twelve battalions were established, manned with able-bodied men aged between twenty-three and thirty-two. They trained twice a year and added their strength to the regular army (now again generally known as *Nizamiye* (Regular), which name was reintroduced officially in 1841) in times of war. The establishment was 57,000 in 1834 and after a reorganization in 1836 grew to 100,000 men. During the nineteenth century the *Redif*'s main task was keeping law and order in the countryside. In conformity with the Prussian regulations of 1814, the *Redif* had its own separate officer corps, whose members at first were drawn from the younger members of the local notable families (who were supposed to take the role of the *Landjunker* in Prussia) and served for two days a week for a salary one-quarter of that of equivalent regular army officers.[5]

Universal conscription on the modern European model began to be discussed towards the end of Mahmud II's reign and there can be no doubt that this time the role model was very much Mehmed Ali, whose well-trained army of conscripted Egyptian peasants had shown its superiority over the *Mansure* army in Syria in 1831–3.

The Military Council (*Dâr-i Şûrâ-yi Askerî*) was established in 1837, and a year later proposed that a five-year term of military service should be introduced and this suggestion was incorporated in the famous Imperial Edict of Gülhane, the reform charter promulgated in 1839. The edict noted that the burden of defence had so far fallen very unequally on different areas and that lifetime service had damaged the population as well as the quality of the army.[6] The passage in question reads:

As regards military matters, for the above-mentioned reasons these are among the most important. Although it is the duty of the subjects to provide soldiers for the defence of the fatherland, it is also true that up to now the size of the population of a province has not been taken into account and because some [provinces] had to provide more [soldiers] than they could, others fewer, this has become the cause of all kinds of disorder and chaos in useful occupations such as agriculture and trade. As life-long service for those who enter the army causes loss of zeal and decline in the population, it is necessary with regard to those soldiers who will be recruited in each province according to need, to establish some good rules and to establish a system of rotation with a term of service of four to five years.

This led to new army regulations, which were promulgated in September 1843 under Rıza Pasha. Primarily inspired by Prussian regulations, with some French influence, they established a regular *Nizamiye* army manned by conscripts (*muvazzaf*), who served for five years (later reduced to four, three and – finally – two years), and a reserve army, manned by those who had completed their service with the regular army and those who had drawn a low number in the *kur'a* (drawing of lots). The term of service in the *Redif* was seven years, during which time the reservists were called up for training for one month a year (this proved too disruptive, so was later changed to once every two years). Each of the five armies into which the Ottoman army was divided – the Guard, Istanbul, the European provinces, Anatolia and the Arab provinces – had its own separate reserve attached to it.[7] The *Redif* continued in this fashion until 1912, when a decision was taken to merge it with the regular army. Due to the upheavals of the Balkan war, the merger only took place in the course of 1914.[8]

The system of conscription was first established in detail under the *Kur'a nizamnamesi* (regulation on the drawing of lots) of 1848. It put the strength of the army at 150,000, which meant that, with five-year service, the army needed to recruit 30,000 volunteers and conscripts a year.

Conscription was done through the drawing of lots among those eligible on the basis of sex, health and age. Those whose names were drawn were drafted into the *Nizamiye* army, while the others were relegated to the *Redif*, without first having to serve with the regular army.

The system remained more or less unchanged until the new army regulations proclaimed in August 1869 under Hüseyin Avni Pasha, whereby the soldiers were divided into three categories: the *nizamiye* (regulars), the *redif* (reserve – *Landwehr*) and the *mustahfız* (guards – *Landsturm*). The regular army was divided into two classes: those men actually under arms for four years, the *muvazzaf*, and those who, having completed their four-year service, were then incorporated for one or two years into the *İhtiyat* (active reserve) to serve in their region of origin, where they apparently acted as a kind of permanent 'backbone' to the local *Redif* battalion. The total active land army of the empire after the changes of 1869 is put at 210,000, 150,000 under arms and 60,000 in the active reserve.

Those who had completed their service with the regular army, those who had been allowed to return to their homes because they were sole breadwinners and those who were over thirty-two years of age served with the *Redif* for a further six years, as did those whose names had not come up to begin with. In 1869, the strength of the reserve was put at being slightly over 190,000.[9]

The *Mustahfiz* reserve was the least active, least well armed part of the army. It was not expected to take the field in time of war, but rather was to take over garrison duties and general law-and-order work when the regular army and the reserve were at the front. It consisted of (relatively) able-bodied men who had done their service in the *Nizamiye* and/or *Redif*. They served for eight years, between the ages of thirty-two and forty. Total strength was 300,000.

In March 1870 the whole system of recruitment was reviewed and codified in a new *kur'a kanunnamesi* (conscription law), published in 1871. This remained the basic set of regulations until after the constitutional revolution of 1908, but some of its provisions were modified during the army reforms of 1879 (after the disastrous defeat in the war against Russia) and those of 1885–7, when the German military advisers led by Colmar, Freiherr von der Goltz, worked in Istanbul.

The law consisted of seventy-seven articles, grouped in seven chapters: general ground rules for the conscription; reasons for exemption from military service; treatment of those who dodged the draft or intended to use trickery to evade military service; execution of the draft; measures to be executed after the draft; conditions for the acceptance of volunteers in the army; and conditions pertaining to the people who sent replacements or paid the exemption tax.

The way the draft should be executed was described in great detail. First, conscription councils were to be formed in each recruiting district (which coincided with the *Redif* districts). Three months before the drawing of lots was to take place, the population records were checked and lists of possible recruits drawn up. All those who figured in the records were then ordered to appear in person in the district capital. After those who could show that they had a right to exemption on the basis of health or other reasons, separated, had been all those who were going to be included in the draft were arranged around a square or open place. Two bags were put in the centre, one filled with envelopes, each containing a small piece of paper with the name of one of the men on it; the other containing an equal number of pieces of paper in envelopes. Depending on the number of recruits needed, that number of slips of paper in the second bag were inscribed with '*asker oldum*' ('I have become a soldier'), the rest being left blank. The envelopes were then taken from the first bag and the names read, one after another, and they were matched with papers from the second bag. This went on until all the slips with '*asker oldum*' on them, had been read.[10] Later legislation, such as the military service law of 1916, is even more detailed and specific. Under article 14 of this law all males who had reached the age of eighteen before 1 March in any given year had to report in person and in the company of their village headman to the authorities in the district capital before the end of October. Recruitment started on 1 May and included all those who had turned twenty before 1 March.[11]

It seems, however, that this regular procedure was not always followed in areas (Albania, Kurdistan) where feudal relationships were strong. According to one report, conscription in Albania was purely a façade and recruits were really selected and sent by their tribal chiefs.[12]

In the reforms of 1879 (which also introduced the division as the basic unit of the army) the term of service with the regular army was brought up to six years, of which three were spent under arms (at least in the infantry) and three in the active reserve. The period of service in the *Redif* was brought down from eight to six years, of which three were classed as *Mukaddem* (vanguard) and three as *Tali* (rear). Service with the *Mustahfiz* was likewise brought down from eight to six years. In 1887 the *Redif* districts were reorganized.

At the end of empire the Young Turks changed the term of service with the regular army again. In 1909 it was brought down from three to two years for those soldiers serving in particularly unhealthy climes: for instance, with the Sixth Army in Iraq and the Seventh in Yemen.[13] With the passing of the last Ottoman conscription law in May 1914, the term was brought down from three to two years for the whole infantry, but, as mobilization started almost immediately afterwards, this measure was largely theoretical.

The problem of exemptions

In introducing conscription as the basis for its recruitment system, the empire of course faced the same problems as European states. Conscription presupposed the existence of a fairly reliable census to determine where the potential manpower could be found. This required a sizeable growth in the state, and especially the provincial, bureaucracy. A census in the strict sense of the word, that is, a population count of the whole empire at one and the same time, remained outside the possibilities of the Ottomans until the very end of the empire. Only the republic was able to introduce it in 1927. The Ottomans had a tradition of population registration, however, and the first one of modern times (counting only male heads of households) was held in the years 1831–8. A second registration, specifically for the purpose of enabling conscription to work, was conducted in 1844. As actual counting was impossible in many areas due to lack of manpower or to popular resistance (particularly on the part of tribes), the results were no more than a rough estimate, and certainly a serious undercount of the population.

European writers working from the 1844 results put the total population of the empire (excluding Africa) at about 32 million, while the much more reliable data from the later nineteenth century, particularly the registration carried out between 1882 and 1890 and published in 1893, give a total of about 17.5 million, which is not entirely incredible given the large losses in land and population suffered during the 1877–8 Russian war, but certainly represents an undercount.[14] For 1914, at the beginning of the last large-scale war ever fought by the Ottomans, the number is put at 18.5 million for the core provinces,[15] or between 23 and 25 million if all of the outlying provinces are included.[16]

The lack of an accurate census made it especially difficult for the Ottoman authorities to get all those who were liable to serve to take part in the draft. Although some wars, such as the 1897 war with Greece and the 1912 Balkan War did arouse enthusiasm in some places, resulting in quite large numbers of volunteers,[17] under normal circumstances military service was very unpopular. This was due primarily to the length of service. The lack of manpower, especially in combination with the attrition caused not so much by the great wars as by never-ending guerrilla warfare, in Albania, Macedonia, the Hawran and above all Yemen, meant that conscripts were very often kept under arms for far longer than their legal term. Some reports speak of conscripts serving for ten years and more.[18] Even when there was initially an enthusiastic response, this tended to evaporate very fast when recruits were faced with conditions in the army.[19] The lack of an industrial base meant that the state had the greatest difficulty in feeding, clothing and equipping its soldiers. Pay was regularly in arrears. The conditions under which the army had to fight in wartime were atrocious. In the 1877–8 Russian war, in the Balkan war of 1912–13 and in World War I, large parts of the army were starving and many more soldiers died of cholera, typhus and dysentery than died of wounds.

In the countryside it was relatively easy to go into hiding, even for those who were registered. 'Leaving for the mountains' to stay out of the hands of the representatives of the state was a well-established tradition in the Ottoman Balkans and Anatolia. Like other countries, therefore, the empire had a system of heavy penalties for draft-dodgers and people who hid or helped them. The regulations adopted in 1909 also included a system of material and personal sureties, whereby those who had no property were required to have a male family member (father, brother or uncle) vouch for them.[20]

What made the manpower problem even more serious was the exceptionally large proportion of the population exempted from military service. Like most countries which introduced conscription, the Ottoman Empire, had a set of regulations about exemptions. Broadly speaking, one can say that there existed two types of exemption: individual and collective. Groups which were exempted were women; non-Muslims (formally until 1856, in practice until 1909); inhabitants of the holy places, Mecca and Medina; religious functionaries and students in religious schools; and a whole range of professional groups. Exemption from the draft was a prime attraction of membership of each of these groups. It is even reported that young men went on pilgrimage to Mecca when recruitment threatened. The regulations of 1871, 1886, 1909 and 1916 all contain provisions about exemptions. The 1916 regulations are particularly specific, with long lists of exempted professions. Some (top civil servants, judges, *mufti*s (Islamic jurisconsults) were exempt under all circumstances, while others (for instance, lower-ranking civil servants, policemen, railway clerks) were exempt except in case of mobilization.[21]

Nomads, even if not legally exempt, by and large were so in practice. Istanbul with its outlying districts (and a population of over a million) also did not deliver a single soldier to the army.[22] The Ottoman army was therefore an army of sedentary Muslim men, and, as over 80 per cent of the population was rural even at the dawn of the twentieth century, primarily one of sedentary Muslim peasants.

Individuals who belonged to those sections of the population which were obliged to serve could claim exemption if they could show that they were *muinsiz* (without support, or sole breadwinner in their household). The actual regulations are quite complicated and interesting as they clearly reflect the realities of life and family relationships of the time, as in this example:

> The father-in-law is not to be considered the supporter of a husband, but he may be so considered in a case where the wife inhabits the home of the father-in-law of her husband [i.e. of her own father].

A young married man whose wife is dead or divorced leaving children is exempted. The care of the latter is the duty of the young father, even though natural supporters of the young woman exist, as, for example, her father, father-in-law and brother. This is in order that the orphans may not be allowed to fall into the hands of the stepmother.[23]

The essential point was that men were considered *muinsiz*, and therefore exempt, if they could not be replaced as breadwinners of their households.[24]

Those who were not without support could escape conscription only by a lucky draw or through payment. Anyone drawing a blank for six years in a row, and so escaping service in the regular army, was enrolled in the reserve, but any Muslim man liable to serve could also buy exemption. The first conscription law of 1848 allowed a conscript to send a personal replacement (*bedel-i şahsî*) – in other words, he could send someone else if he could force, persuade or pay anyone to go in his place – but the 1870 regulations, while still mentioning personal replacement as a possibility, also detail the way in which service could be bought off. Exemption could be bought for 5000 kuruş or 50 gold lira (a very considerable sum at the time). Those seeking exemption were not allowed to sell land, house or tools in order to pay.[25]

This payment, called *bedel-i nakdî* (cash payment-in-lieu) in the sources, should not be confused with the – much lower – sums paid by non-Muslims until 1909. Those who had bought their exemption, like those who drew a lucky lot, were declared reservists, until a change in the law in May 1914, which stipulated that they should serve for six months with the active army and only then be classified as reservists. The same law made the *bedel* applicable in peacetime only, but it seems doubtful that the Ottoman government, always hungry for money, actually suspended the practice during World War I. The regulations for payment of the *bedel* also found their way into the first military service law of the republic (of 1927), but by then the amount was determined as 600 lira.[26]

With the famous exception of the Janissary corps, which had been recruited from among the Christian peasantry (but whose members converted to Islam), primarily in the European provinces, the empire had only rarely employed non-Muslims for its land forces. Traditionally the bearing of arms had been the prerogative of the ruling elite, the *askerî* (military) servants of the Sultan, and when lack of manpower forced the government to start arming members of the subject class (*reaya*), in the form of irregulars (*levend*) drawn from the peasantry and the town roughs, this use was again confined to Muslims.

The Reform Edict of Gülhane, the first conscription law of 1844 and the regulations of 1871 all specified that all Muslims (*bilcümle ahaliyi müslime*) were liable to serve in the army. At that time, the idea that non-Muslims should be allowed, or forced, to serve seems to have been as alien as the idea of female soldiers. But the reform edict which 'Ali Pasha drew up in 1856 in close cooperation with the French and British ambassadors, and which formed the empire's entry ticket to the 'Concert of Europe', emphasized equality between Muslims and non-Muslims. Application of this principle meant that the dicriminatory practice of conscription would have to cease and non-Muslims would have to take part in the drawing of lots as well.[27] In reality, there was very little enthusiasm for the idea on either side. The army feared that an intake of Christian peasants would be a burden to it and that non-Muslims would damage morale. This was a serious point, because, as all observers of the Ottoman army between 1850 and 1918 agree, the fighting spirit of the Ottoman troops was to a very high degree religious. Attacks were always carried out to shouts of 'Allah, Allah' and 'Allahüekber' (God is great). It would be hard to envisage a religiously mixed army doing the same. Most Muslims, especially in the countryside, disliked the idea of Christians bearing arms (one observer compares their feelings to those in the southern United States on the equality of blacks).[28]

Most Ottoman Christians were equally unenthusiastic. By and large they felt themselves to be subjects of the Ottoman state, not members of an Ottoman nation. The idea of Ottoman nation-building (known at the time as the idea of the 'Unity of the Elements') always was limited to a small, mostly Muslim, elite.

The Ottoman government, finally, had the strongest incentive of all not actually to conscript Christians. The emphasis on equality before the law in the 1856 edict also meant that the *cizye* tax, which Christians and Jews traditionally paid as a tribute to the Islamic state in which they lived, had to go. Although the number of Ottoman Christians went down considerably during the last century of the empire due to the loss of European provinces, they still represented nearly 30 per cent of the population in Abdülhamid's reign and close to 20 per cent on the eve of World War I; the *cizye* was the state's second most important source of tax revenue (after the tithe) of the state. No wonder, then, that the state actually preferred that the Christians should pay an exemption tax (called first *iane-i askerî* – military assistance – and then *bedel-i askerî* – military payment-in-lieu) of their own, rather than serve. This indeed remained universal practice until 1909. The *bedel* was much lower than that required of Muslims and, like the *cizye* before it, was paid collectively by Christian and Jewish communities to tax-farmers and, later, salaried treasury officials.

That the recruitment of Christian subjects into the army was never a serious option before 1909 is shown clearly by the text of the 1870 regulations. Its first article reads: 'All the Muslim population of the Well-protected domains of His Majesty are personally obliged to fulfil the military service which is incumbent on them.' There is no mention of non-Muslims, which clearly suggests that in the Ottomans' eyes they did not come within the compass of the military service law.

Military service for non-Christians thus remained a theoretical option until 1909. This is not to say that there were no Christians in the army – there were, but they were officers, primarily in the medical corps, which consisted for a large part of Armenian and Greek army doctors who held the ranks of lieutenant and captain.

The Young Turks, who came to power in July 1908 and for whom unity and equality between the different ethnic 'elements' of the empire were a top priority, started work on the change of the recruitment law soon after they had suppressed the counter-revolution of April 1909 in Istanbul. In July 1909 military service was made compulsory for all Ottoman subjects. At the same time a number of Muslim groups – for instance, students in religious colleges who had failed their exams, but also the inhabitants of Istanbul – lost their exempt status. In October 1909, the recruitment of conscripts irrespective of religion was ordered for the first time.[29]

The reactions of the Christian communities to the new law were mixed. There was no enthusiasm. The spokesmen of the Greek, Syrian, Armenian and Bulgarian communities – in other words, the members of the elite – agreed in principle, but with the all-important proviso that the members of their communities serve in separate, ethnically uniform, units officered by Christians. The Bulgarians also insisted on serving in the European provinces only.[30] This was totally unacceptable to the Young Turks, who saw it as just another way to boost the centrifugal forces of nationalism in the empire – the opposite of what they were aiming for. At grass-roots level, many young Christian men, especially Greeks, who could afford it and who had the overseas connections, opted to leave the country or at least to get a foreign passport.[31] Those who could not leave, change their nationality, or pay the much higher *bedel-i nakdî* (along with well-to-do Muslims), were indeed recruited when World War I broke out, but the Ottoman government continued to mistrust its Christian subjects to such an extent that almost without exception they were left unarmed. Instead they served in labour battalions, doing repair work on the roads and railways and, especially, carrying supplies to the front.

The result of the extensive system of exemptions was that the empire, already far less populous than its rivals, drew fewer conscripts from its relatively small population as well. Its yearly required intake of recruits in 1913–14 (when the term of service was still three years) was 70,000 or about 0.35 per cent of the population. In reality the intake was probably lower. In Bulgaria the ratio at that time was 0.75 per cent. Fully mobilized, as in early 1915, only 4 per cent of the population was under arms and on active duty, compared with, for instance, 10 per cent in France.[32] The true strength of the army on the eve of World War I is not altogether clear, but it is certain that it was relatively small by contemporary continental European standards. A report by the British military attaché in January 1910 gives the nominal peacetime strength as 300,000 and the term of service in the regular army as three years. This means that 100,000 recruits per year were needed, but the actual annual contingent was put at 90,000, of whom, after exemptions, 50,000 were enrolled. This meant that the actual peacetime establishment was only about 150,000 and the inclusion of large numbers of *Redif*s was necessary to bring the army up to strength. A British report written in 1914 puts the peacetime strength of the army at 230,000 before the Balkan wars and 200,000 thereafter. Larcher, on the other hand, states that in 1914 the active army was composed of two classes of about 90,000 each, which would mean an army of between 180,000 and 200,000 men.[33] The peacetime establishment of the Russian army (which also recruited a low percentage of the population, but could afford it because of the sheer size of that population) was five times its size in the early twentieth century. The Austrian army was at least twice the size of the Ottoman one.[34]

When fully mobilized, the Ottoman army was of course much bigger – that, after all, was the main advantage of the conscription system – but mobilization was painfully slow, taking four to five months to complete (if transport to the front is included). The mass mobilizations of 1912 and 1914 showed up all the inherent weaknesses in the Ottoman system. The slow mobilization of 1912 (due mainly to lack of good roads, but also to confusion and the inability of the armies to absorb, equip and feed the reservists) meant that the Balkan war had been lost before the troops from the Asiatic provinces even reached the European fronts. With only one single-track railway available for supplies and troop movements, the troops at the front (only thirty miles from Istanbul for most of the war!) were starving and when the Syrian reserves finally arrived the cholera they brought with them killed thousands of soldiers. At the outset of the war, though there seems to have been little enthusiasm, there was nevertheless a genuine and quite widespread readiness to serve, but it evaporated quickly under the harsh circumstances. Even during the first days of marching after leaving their depots, supplies ran out and the troops had to live off the land; Large-scale desertion started.[35]

The outbreak of World War I in 1914 again saw a very slow process of mobilization (even slower than that of the Russians). This time it had to take place in winter, which made the whole process more burdensome, especially in eastern Anatolia. On the other hand, warfare was practically impossible in winter on the Caucasian front and, if Enver Pasha had not squandered 72,000 soldiers' lives (out of 90,000) by ordering an attack over the mountain passes at Sarıkamış, the Ottoman army could have been at full war strength in the spring. Once again, the call to arms was answered relatively well, in Anatolia if not in the Arab provinces, but as in the Balkan war, the conditions in the army (payment with worthless paper money, undernourishment, lack of medical care, epidemics of typhus, cholera and dysentery, bad or non-existent clothing and shoes) were so bad, that desertions soon started to become a problem of enormous proportions. By the end of the war the number of deserters was four times that of soldiers on the front.[36]

The conclusion would seem to be that the Ottomans, over a period of sixty years and as part of a more general programme of modernization, managed to put in place quite a sophisticated system of recruitment through conscription modelled on that of Prussia/Germany, but that by the early twentieth century the lack of infrastructure and an industrial base meant that they could not really cope with the mass army they had so diligently created.

Conscription failed as an instrument of Ottoman nation-building, too. The system of exemptions through the *bedel-i nakdî* and the *bedel-i askerî* meant that the burden never fell equally on all Ottoman subjects. Even at the end, the Ottoman army remained an army of Anatolian Muslim peasants, in a sense foreshadowing the establishment of a Turkish nation-state in Anatolia after World War I.

Notes

1 On the reign of Selim III, see Stanford J. Shaw, *Between Old and New: The Ottoman Empire under Selim III, 1789–1807* (Cambridge, MA, 1971). On Selim's fall, see *Between Old and New*, p. 345 ff. On the *Nizam-i Cedid* army, see Stanford J. Shaw, 'The Origins of Ottoman Military Reform: the Nizam-i Cedid Army of Sultan Selim III', *Journal of Modern History* 37 (1965), pp. 291–306.

2 See Chapter 9 in this volume.

3 See Chapter 3 in this volume.

4 Mahmud II's army reforms are described in Stanford J. Shaw, *History of the Ottoman Empire and Modern Turkey*, vol. 2, *Reform, Revolution and Republic: The Rise of Modern Turkey 1808–1975* (Cambridge, 1977), pp. 41–5, and in Fahri Çoker, 'Tanzimat ve Ordudaki Yenilikler', in Murat Belge, ed., *Tanzimattan Cumhuriyete Türkiye Ansiklopedisi* (6 vols., Istanbul, 1985), vol. 5, pp. 1260–66.

5 Jean Deny, 'Redif', in *Encyclopaedia of Islam. New Edition* (9 vols, Leiden, 1995, vol. 8., pp. 370–71.

6 There are several editions of the Edict of Gülhane. I used [?] Petermann (with Ramis Efendi), *Beiträge zu einer Geschichte der neuesten Reformen des Osmanischen Reiches, enthaltend den Hattischerif von Gülhane, den Ferman von 21 November 1839 und das neueste Strafgesetzbuch* (Berlin, 1842). The quote is taken from pp. 11–12.

7 'Redif', in *İslâm Ansiklopedisi*, vol. 9 (Istanbul, 1971), pp. 666–8.

8 Deny, 'Redif', gives 31 August 1912 as the date of the decision to abolish the *Redif*, on the authority of the official collection of Ottoman legislation known as *Düstur*, vol. 4, p. 615.

9 Murat Belge, ed., *Tanzimattan Cumhuriyete Türkiye Ansiklopedisi* (6 vols Istanbul, 1985), vol. 5, p. 1263.

10 *Qur'a qânûnnâme-i humâyûnu* (Istanbul, 1286/1870–71), parts 1 and 4.

11 *Mükellefiyet-i askeriye qânûn-u muvaqqatı* (Istanbul, 1332/1916), articles 14 and 21.

12 PRO/FO 195/2323: report of 20 June 1909 by military attaché, Constantinople (H. Conyers Surtees).

13 FO/PRO/2323: report by military attaché, Constantinople, of 28 May 1909.

14 Kemal Karpat, *Ottoman Population 1830–1914. Demographic and Social Characteristics* (Madison, WI, 1985); Justin McCarthy, *The Arab World, Turkey and the Balkans: A Handbook of Historical Statistics* (Boston, 1982); Nuri Akbayar, 'Tanzimat'tan Sonra Osmanlı Devleti Nüfusu', in Murat Belge, ed., *Tanzimattan Cumhuriyete Türkiye Ansiklopedisi* (6 vols, Istanbul, 1985), vol. 5, pp. 1238–46.

15 Stanford J. Shaw, 'The Ottoman Census System and Population', *International Journal of Middle East Studies* 9 (1978), pp. 325–38.

16 Ahmed Emin [Yalman], *Turkey in the World War* (New Haven, 1930), p. 79.

17 See, for instance, Ömer Sami Coşar's biography of Atatürk's bodyguard, *Atatürk'ün Muhafızı Topal Osman* (n.p, n.d), p. 5, describing recruitment in Giresun. However, when the British consuls reported on the reactions to mobilization in their stations at the request of the Committee of Imperial Defence (request by Sir Maurice Hankey, secretary to the CID, dated 25 October 1912), they described a very patchy response: Salonica was 'prompt', Gallipoli 'sullen', Izmit 'willing', Adana 'unwilling', Adalia (Antalya) 'reluctant' and Alexandretta (Iskenderun) 'prompt and willing' (FO/PRO 195/2445, pp. 260–322).

18 PRO/FO 195/2346 Report by military attaché, Constantinople (Tyrrell), of 10 April 1910. The same general picture emerges from many eyewitness reports.

19 Reports by the British consuls in Damascus and Antalya are illustrative. The consul in Damascus, in his report of 7 December 1912, says that in the first weeks of October there was much enthusiasm to go to the war, and 60–70 per cent of Muslims presented themselves. But after reverses, and because of bad treatment, enthusiasm dropped and by the end of October only 30 per cent of Muslims responded. People started to flee and hide. Of a company of 130 regulars sent from Damascus to Aleppo, 40 deserted on the way (PRO/FO 195/2445, pp. 291, 311).

20 PRO/FO 195/2323. Report from embassy Constantinople containing a summary of the new recruitment law in translation.

21 *Mükellefiyet-i Askeriye Qânûn-u Muvaqqatı* (1916 conscription law), Articles 91, 92.

22 Ahmet İzzet [Furgaç], *Denkwürdigkeiten des Marschalls Izzet Pascha* (Leipzig, 1927), p. 169.

23 PRO/FO 195/2323, report of 26 September 1909.

24 For a full discussion, see Chapter 5 in this volume.

25 *Qur'a qânûnnâme-i humâyûnu* (Istanbul: Matba'a-i Âmire, 1286/1870–71), Article 70.

26 H. Bowen, 'Bedel', in *Encyclopaedia of Islam. New Edition* (9 vols., Leiden, 1960), vol. 1, p. 855.

27 Roderic H. Davison, *Reform in the Ottoman Empire 1856–1876* (New York, 1973; reprint of 1963 edn.), pp. 94–5.

28 PRO/FO 195/2323, report of 20 June 1909.

29 At this time, the measure may well have been largely symbolic. In 1912 only 5 per cent of those liable to serve seem to have answered the call (PRO/FO 195/2445, p. 291) and according to one report (PRO/FO 195/2456/60, annual military report, Constantinople) no Christians were called up in 1914.

30 PRO/FO 195/2323, report of 20 June 1909.

31 According to reports from Gallipoli and Rhodes in 1912 (PRO/FO 195/2445, pp. 275, 363).

32 Maurice Larcher, *La Guerre turque dans la guerre mondiale* (Paris, 1926), pp. 589–90.

33 PRO/FO 195/2346, report of 17 January 1910, p. 126; PRO/FO 195/2456/60, report of 1914; Larcher, p. 590.

34 F. Schrader et al., *Atlas de la géographie moderne* (Paris, 1914), maps 28, 33.

35 There are quite a few eyewitness reports from the Turkish side of the front in the Balkan War. Among the best are Ellis Ashmead-Bartlett, *With the Turks in Thrace* (London, 1913), and Lionel James, *With the Conquered Turk: The Story of a Latter-Day Adventurer* (London, [1913]).

36 Erik Jan Zürcher, 'Between Death and Desertion. The Ottoman Army in World War I', *Turcica* 28 (1996), pp. 235–58.

5· Taking Care of Soldiers' Families: The Ottoman State and the *Muinsiz alle maaşı*

Nicole A.N.M. van Os

In recent years there has been renewed interest in the study of the Great War. New books and articles have appeared, stressing not the military aspects of the war but its effects on society. Many discuss the effects of World War I on women and on gender. They touch upon the way women's lives changed because of the war. They discuss women's participation in the war – as nurses, as part of the military machinery, as workers in munition factories, as mothers of soldiers – and the effects their participation had on their family life and male–female relationships. Some authors regard the war as a period in which women gained the opportunity to demand more forcefully their social, political and civil rights. The literature that appeared during the period is also an object of study. Some scholars discuss the way women were used as symbols in wartime discourses. Others study the way female writers reflected the war in their works.

However, most of these publications focus on women in Europe or the Anglo-Saxon world. Little has been written on how women outside these areas were affected by the war. This chapter aims to fill the gap, if only in a small way, by discussing one aspect of the war's effects on Ottoman women.

I look at the way the Ottoman state took care of those who needed its support because their son, father or other male relative had been drafted into the army and was actively serving his country.[1] The discussion is limited to 1912–18, during which period the Ottoman Empire became involved first in a war with its neighbours in the Balkans and subsequently in World War I. First, I present the official regulations, tracing them back to the late nineteenth century. Then I discuss the problems that arose during the execution of the rules and the effects of these problems on women and their families. The authorities' efforts to resolve these problems and the combined efforts of civil and governmental organizations to deal with the consequences of the problems, however limited, will also be dealt with. This way I aim to contribute to the knowledge of the effects of war on women and their families in a pre-industrial, largely agricultural country.

Laws and regulations

In his chapter on the reforms of the Ottoman army between 1844 and 1918, Erik Jan Zürcher refers to people who were exempted from military service, among them the so-called *muinsiz*. According to Mehmet Zeki Pakalın, *muinsiz* 'is a term used for a person who does not have have anybody to look after his mother, or, if married, his wife';[2] in short, for a breadwinner.

As Zürcher has explained, although the *muinsiz* were exempt from military service in the regular troops (*nizamiye* and *ihtiyatiye*), they were enlisted in the reserve troops as *redif* and later, after fulfilling their duties as *redif*, as *mustahfiz*. This meant that in case of war or mobilization they, too, were called up and their dependants were left without a breadwinner. In order not to leave such families without any support, the Ottoman state introduced special provisions for them. The way the families were cared for in practice remains unclear, however.

In the law of October/November 1886 in which the *asakir nizam-namesi* (military regulation) is further explained and worked out, there is a special section listing those who were exempt from regular military service.[3] Among them were men who had sole responsibility for the support of relatives. Factors such as the degree of kinship to those left behind, their age, their sex, their physical and mental healths and the availability of other relatives to look after them determined whether someone was exempted from active military service.[4]

For the period after the Young Turk Revolution of 1908 more information is available. For new recruiting law of 1909 a list was compiled of those who were exempted from military service in the regular army, in the same way as in the *nizamname* of 1886.[5] What to do with the families of these *muinsiz* in case of mobilization was worked out in a separate *ad hoc* law passed on the occasion of the mobilization for the Balkan wars. An official circular containing this (provisional) law, dated 19 December 1912, dealt with the allowances to be given to the families of *taht-ı silaha alınan muinsiz efrad-ı redife ve mustahfiz*, breadwinner reservist soldiers who were being called up. The law consisted of only three articles, which stated that the family of a *muinsiz* was to receive an allowance of 30 kuruş per month from 1 Teşrinievvel 1328 (14 October 1912) until the first of the month following the month in which the soldier was discharged. The money for this allowance was to come out of a special provision within the national budget, and the Ministry of Finance was responsible for the execution of the law. In the circular, the law was followed by seventeen points of instructions for the authorities on how to execute the law.[6]

The law was passed by the government in December 1912 and published in the *Takvim-i Vekayi*, the Ottoman official gazette, on 5 February 1913.[7] Even before its publication, the government had decided that the categories of people qualifying for an allowance should be broader, and a day later *Takvim-i Vekay* carried a supplement to the law, saying that an allowance would be paid not only to the families of *muinsiz efrad-ı redife ve mustahfiza*, but also to the families of *muinsiz efrad-ı ihtiyatiye* (breadwinner reservists in the standing army) and the families of regulars and reservists who after having taken up arms had become *muinsiz* (sole breadwinners) but who nevertheless had to serve until the end of the war.[8] To fund the allowances a special fund of 10 million kuruş was created in the budget of the year 1329 (1913–14).[9] Over the years large sums were allocated to this special budget several times.[10]

In the months following the introduction of the law, however, the people charged with its implementation at a local level met so many problems in the interpretation that they wrote to the central authorities asking for further explanations in the specific cases. The Ministry of War and the Ministry of the Interior regularly corresponded on these questions, trying to formulate answers to them and relaying the answers back to the local authorities. The correspondence creates the impression that the law was not always regarded as fair and emphasizes the problems that arose because of its *ad hoc* character.[11]

With the new Provisional Law on Military Service, issued in May 1914, the institution of allowances for soldier's families became more deeply embedded in the system. Many articles of this law were revised in the two following years and in 1916 a new version was published.[12] Some of articles 49–55, which contained the rules on 'soldier's families in need of support', were modified in July and August 1915.[13] According-ing to Article 49 of this provisional law, a family in need of support would get that (financial) support from the moment the soldier concerned had enlisted at the place he was supposed to until the end of the month in which the soldier was discharged. The allowance to be given was to be 30 kuruş a month per person. The same would go for the families of those reservists (efrad-ı mezune, ihtiyatiye ve mustahfıza) who served for more than forty-five days. Those who had a right to this financial support were to be exempted from any administrative costs related to obtaining the support.[14] This article remained the same in the two versions.[15]

Article 50 (appendices I and II) provided a graph of those who were potentially entitled to an allowance and of those who might be appointed as substitute breadwinner (muin) for them. Whether the relatives were regarded as muin also depended on the geographical distance between the potential substitute breadwinner and those in need of support. The father or, in some cases, the well-to-do mother was to replace the breadwinner only if they lived in the same district (kaza); a child, brother, grandfather or father-in-law only if they lived in the same village (kariye) or the same neighbourhood (mahalle); and the remaining candidates only if they lived in the same household (hane).[16] The article had been modified in June 1915 on the initiative of the Ministry of War, which was of the opinion that well-to-do mothers should be included in the list of potential breadwinners. After the change had been approved by the highest religious authority, the Sheyhülislam or Grand Mufti, as being in accordance with Islamic Law, a three-article law was issued, in which Article 50 of the Provisional Law on Military Service had been modified. According to the modification, well-to-do mothers were recognized as breadwinners for their unmarried daughters and for their sons under the age of sixteen if they were living in the same district as these dependants.[17] Moreover, the father-in-law of the wife (wives) of the soldier (that is, the soldier's father) was included as a potential breadwinner for his daughter(s)-in-law.

Article 51 stated that a breadwinner had to be over eighteen and that he or she had to be financially able to fulfil her or his duty. However, for fathers who were appointed breadwinner there was an extra precondition: they also had to be physically healthy.[18] This part of the article, too, had been revised. Before the revision (of 9 August 1915) the precondition of physical and financial strength had counted indiscriminately for all potential breadwinners.[19] In both versions of the article students at boarding-schools, prisoners, soldiers in arms and those of whom it was unknown whether they were alive or dead were excluded from being breadwinners.[20] The remaining articles, 52 to 55, had not been changed. According to Article 52 the persons in the graph were to be considered in need of support only if they did not have any of the relatives mentioned as potential breadwinners in the graph, if their yearly income was insufficient for their livelihood according to the local market prices of the district, and if they did not work in the agricultural, trade or arts sector. It also stated that any salary or allowance would be regarded as income and that the wealth and income of the soldier in arms would be considered the wealth and income of the relatives in need of help. Furthermore, it declared that applications for an allowance would be considered by the recruitment centres. Those who were declared to have the right to support would be put under the protection of the municipality or the local committee of elders. The civil authorities would also take care of the possessions of those soldiers who had no relatives to look after them.[21]

Article 53 required that the soldier on active duty had been caring for those applying for the allowance and it limited the number of people anyone would have to care for to one person outside his own immediate family (*aile*). If he/she was a potential *muin* for more than one person, then he/she was to choose one. The others had to be cared for by the next on the list or, if there were none left, were to be given the state allowance.[22]

The last two articles, 54 and 55, were related to the administrative handling of the allowances.[23]

However, even with the changes introduced in July and August 1915, these articles were not sufficient to deal with all the complex situations created by the war. The authorities charged with the execution of the law continued to refer regularly to the central authorities with questions on the exact interpretation of the law.

In October 1915 it was decided that a separate law on the *muinsiz aile maaşı* ('Allowance for Families without a Breadwinner', or separation allowance) was needed. The bill for this law was discussed in the Council of State.[24] Taking the 1914 Temporary Law on Military Service as a starting-point, the articles were modified according to the ideas of the council members. The new law had thirty-one articles, in which the allowance was regulated in more detail than before. The changes related to issues such as which soldiers were eligible to be declared *muinsiz*, what to do with the families of soldiers on (sick-)leave, deserters, prisoners of war, those whose whereabouts were unknown and casualties of war. The changes seem to have been aimed at answering the questions of the local authorities about problems with the interpretation of the old rules. Furthermore, the articles on who could be appointed a substitute breadwinner were revised, with a broadening of the category of *muin*, perhaps in order to alleviate the financial burden of the state. For example, a person could now be a substitute breadwinner for three persons besides his wife, children and parents, instead of just one.[25] On the other hand, the number of dependants was increased: more relatives could now ask for support than under the earlier regulations. A difference was made between the allowances for those living in Istanbul and those living elsewhere, there was now a maximum allowance per family equal to the allowances of five persons. Other modifications related to the implications of changes in the family situation, to the question of what to do with the lands of *muinsiz* in arms, and to the administration of the allowances.

In short, this bill contained much more detail, to help the local authorities cope with the questions and problems which had resulted from the lack of clarity of the former law.[26] More clarity, however, did not mean that the system became more adequate.

The implementation of the regulations

Although the Ottoman government had set all these rules to provide the families of its soldiers with a basic income, the system was by no means adequate. There were several reasons for this.

The allowance the families got was an allowance in cash. The allowance *per capita* was set at 30 kuruş per month with a maximum per family of 150 kuruş. The Council of State suggested raising this figure for those living within the borders of the Greater Municipality of Istanbul to 40 kuruş per person per month in 1915, leaving it at 30 kuruş per person per month for those living elsewhere.[27] Due to the financial situation of the Ottoman Empire, however, a proposal to increase the allowances made in April 1917 had to be rejected.[28]

But while the allowances remained unchanged, the price of food soared during the war years, especially during the later years of World War I. Between 1914 and 1918 the price of one *okka* (approximately 1250 grams) of rice rose from 3 to 95 kuruş in Istanbul. The price of sugar increased even more: from 3 to 140 kuruş.[29] Bread could hardly be found and was of very poor quality.[30]

The main reason for the price increases was the shortage of food on the market, for which there were several reasons. The first was a drop in agricultural production within the Ottoman Empire. Temporary decreases were caused by natural disasters such as earthquakes, draughts or plagues of locusts. A more structural reason for the fall in agricultural production was the lack of manpower due to the mobilization. The government took several measures in order to try to maintain, and later to increase, production. As early as December 1912, regulations were issued in order to ensure that the families of men who had been called up continued production. According to these regulations, the land of *muinsiz* families was to be sown by other farmers under the supervision of the local committee of elders. If there were too few farmers in the district to take care of the *muinsiz* families' land, the committee of elders would ask for workers to assist on the farms. The same method was to be employed if an appointed 'breadwinner' (*muin*) for a family was unable to do all the work for himself and his dependants. If the farmers had no seed to sow, or had no money with which to purchase it, this would be provided by the agricultural banks as soon as possible. Supervision of the crops in the fields was the responsibility of the committee of elders, too. If necessary they had to appoint guards who not only had to make sure that the crops were not stolen or illegally harvested, but also had to prevent animals from eating them. These arrangements were to be supervised by the Agricultural Chambers (*Ziraat Odaları*).[31]

Despite these measures, agricultural production declined sharply after the beginning of World War I, and further action was needed to restore production levels. With the help of the Germans, irrigation works were developed and areas which had been left barren were cultivated again. A (Provisional) Law on Agricultural Service was issued in September 1916[32] and passed by the Senate on 10 April 1917.[33] Under this law all men and women who had been working in the agricultural sector, who were not liable for military service and who were over fourteen years of age were to be allocated by the Ministry of Agriculture to work in the agricultural sector.[34] In a regulation of October 1917 this was worked out in more detail. The number of plough-oxen of a farmer determined how much land he had to cultivate. The area cultivated in turn determined the number of persons who could be exempted from regular military service and become third-class reservists (*mustahfız*) in order to be able to cultivate that plot. The regulation also stated that land left uncultivated because of lack of manpower was to be taken over by the village authorities.[35] In cases of lack of manpower, the needy families of soldiers,[36] prisoners of war, and non-Muslim soldiers in special worker's battalions were employed,[37] while the authorities in Niğde asked the authorities in Istanbul for permission to let civil servants work in the agricultural sector for one month during harvest time.[38] In May 1917, Cemal Pasha, the commander of the Syrian armies, also formed special workers' battalions, consisting of women, within the Fourth Army,[39] while in September 1917 other special Women Workers' Battalions were formed by the Kadınları Çalıştırma Cemiyet-i İslamiyesi (Islamic Society for the Employment of Women).[40] By 1918, the need for agricultural labour had increased so much that those convicted of minor offences were also employed during the harvest.[41]

Although by these means the government initially succeeded in increasing agricultural production, the food did not reach the people in the towns or cities, nor were the people in the rural areas able to obtain or keep enough for themselves. Most of the produce was handed over as (special) taxes to provide not only the Ottoman army but also those of its allies with the necessary food.[42] The heavy tax burden was reason for some women to complain to the authorities.[43] The local officials in turn applied to the Ministry of Interior with requests to spare the people in their district, because, as they pointed out, a higher tax burden would lead to starvation of women and children.[44] The governor (mutasarrıf) of Izmit pointed out that, although some of the families in his district had been able to produce enough food for themselves, they still needed an allowance to meet their other needs. He therefore asked the authorities not to cut their allowance as they had planned to.[45] According to the regulations, however, the families were allowed to keep an amount of grain based on an allocation of 500 grams per day. The remainder had to be handed over as tax.[46]

Apart from natural disasters, lack of manpower and the needs of the army, other causes of high food prices were hoarding and profiteering: merchants kept food in stock instead of bringing it onto the market, thus driving up prices. The government tried to prevent this by decentralized control: in February 1916 it asked the local authorities to take charge of food distribution, allocating £100,000 Turkish to each municipality.[47] In May 1916 it authorized the local authorities to determine the price of bread.[48] Obviously, this was not sufficient, because in July 1916 it founded a central distribution committee, the Central Committee for Public Foodsupply (İaşe-yi Umumiye Merkez

Heyeti), supervised by representatives from the Ministry of Interior, the Ministry of War, the Ministry of Finance and that of Trade, and from the General Directorate of the Agricultural Bank. The Ministry of Finance allocated £3.5 million Turkish to the committee to fund the food distribution.[49] Even these measures were not very successful. It was only when, at the end of the war, the banks stopped giving traders credit based on their stocks, that they were forced to sell their hoarded goods and prices fell somewhat. However, by that time most people had exhausted whatever capital they had had.

The inadequacy of the separation allowance was exacerbated by the fact that payment was often unreliable. Some cases of corruption were reported,[50] but in general the reason for the non-payment was lack of money at the local and the national level. The provincial administrators regularly sent demands to Istanbul for more money, complaining that they were unable to pay the allowances on time.[51] Towards the end of World War I, the situation got progressively worse. People were reported as eating grass or simply starving.[52] Because of high inflation and a widespread lack of confidence in paper money, local officials asked the central authorities to send not paper money but copper coins, or even to turn the cash allowance into an allowance in kind.[53] They were incited to do so by the families involved, who gave voice to their complaints by sending telegrams to the local authorities or by simply rebelling. The latter was the case in Aydın, for example, where in March 1916 a group of soldiers' families attacked a bakery and beat up the official in charge of the allowances because they had received no money for three months. The government, fearing the spread of the unrest to other areas, decided to send £20,000 Turkish.[54] Most women, however, tried to convince the authorities of their pitiful situation by more peaceful means.

Consequences and solutions

In the central archives there are many telegrams from women complaining about the increasingly difficult situation, not only for themselves but often also on behalf of all the soldiers' families in the village or neighbourhood. They claimed their right to government support, which right, they said, was based not on their position as women in need of money and food, but on their identity as the wives, daughters and mothers of men who had taken up arms in order to fulfil the holy duty of defending the faith and the fatherland.

These telegrams were sent from all over the empire, showing that the situation was equally bad everywhere. The women living in Istanbul with their families, on the other hand, can hardly be traced in the records of the Ministry of Interior. There may be various reasons for this. One possibility is that their letters or telegrams would end up not at the Ministry of Interior but at a lower level such as, for example, the *vilayet* (province). If that is the case, further research may one day unearth the telegrams. Another possibility is that their situation was relatively better, though this seems unlikely in view of the accounts in some of the autobiographical works available.[55] On the other hand, the women in the city did have more opportunities to find a way out of a seemingly hopeless situation. The lack of manpower made it possible for women to obtain jobs within the lower bureaucratic levels or the service sector. Moreover, in Istanbul quite a few (women's) organizations were active, providing help for those in need. Although many of them only provided food, others tried to give women a chance to work and earn their living.

Some of these women's organizations were founded by foreigners. The wife of the British ambassador, Lady Lowther, founded an organization which collected money in order to help the families of soldiers and the refugees who arrived in Istanbul as a result of the Balkan wars. By the end of March 1913 the organization had distributed food and goods to 8700 soldiers' families and 16,000 refugees. With the £7000 sterling left, she planned to open workshops in Bebek, Eyüp and Üsküdar where the widows and orphans of the war casualties could earn a living.[56] However, it is not clear whether the workshops were actually founded. In June 1913 she had to return to Britain and, although she asked the Municipality of Istanbul to take over her work, there are no indications that this happened.[57] The wives of the French and Dutch ambassadors, too, were active in charity work for the refugees of the Balkan wars and World War I.[58]

In addition, Ottoman women founded organizations aimed at helping specifically those women who were left without male relatives to care for them. Some of these organizations were private, in the sense that they were founded on the initiative of private persons. Organizations such as the Mamulat-i Dahiliye İstihlâkı Kadınlar Cemiyet-i Hayriyesi (Charitable Women's Organization for the Consumption of Local Products), the Osmanlı Türk Kadınları Esirgeme Derneği (Ottoman Turkish Club for the Protection of Women) and the Türk Kadınları Biçki Yurdu (Turkish Women's Tailoring Centre) fall in this category.

They all set up courses and workshops where poor women and girls were taught an honourable job with which they could earn a living. Other organizations were semi-official, being founded at the instigation or under the protection of a state institution. For example, the Asker Aileleri Yardımcı Hanımlar Cemiyeti (Ladies' Society for Assistance to Soldiers' Families) and the Islamic Society for the Employment of Women were both connected with the Ministry of War. The former was founded on the initiative of the daughters of Feldmarschall Liman von Sanders in January 1915, its founding members being the wives of prominent members of the Ottoman establishment.[59] Its main aim was, as its name indicates, to help the families of soldiers, mainly through the distribution of food. The organization reached its target groups by advertising in the newspapers: soldiers' families in need of food were requested to come to certain places to register. Within a few weeks of its foundation the organization was reported to have distributed oil, rice, beans and salt to more than 5000 persons belonging to 2095 families.[60] Its members were more than once rewarded with medals of the Red Crescent.[61] It goes without saying, however, that at the end of World War I, the German members withdrew from the organization.[62]

The Islamic Society for the Employment of Women was founded in June 1916 by Enver Pasha, whose wife princess Naciye Sultan was made its patroness. According to Article 2 of its statutes, it was founded 'to protect women by finding work for them and by accustoming them to earning an honourable living'.[63] A look at the figures given in an annual report published in 1918 reveals that the society was filling a need: in the month and a half after it started its activities on 14 August 1916 more than 14,000 women applied for jobs in its workshops, where mainly textile-related goods were produced. At the three branches the society opened, women were employed to work both in the workshops and at home. Between October 1916 and December 1917 the society claimed to have paid a total of £7,617 Turkish to 24,254 daily workers. This figure, however, is exaggerated, because of the way the number was calculated: the reporters determined the number of employees for each separate month and then totalled these numbers. Thus someone who had been employed for half a year would have been counted six times.[64] Edhem Nejat, without giving any source, said that by October 1918 the society had educated and employed 56,000 women.[65] However, even if these figures are exaggerated, they still indicate that there was a great need for such opportunities for women.

Besides these two organizations, the Hilâl-i Ahmer Cemiyeti (Red Crescent Society), which can be regarded as a semi-official organization, aimed at helping women in need. It also employed women in the textile workshops it opened from 1915. By 1917 it was employing 200 women full-time, while 300 others worked only two days a week. The women produced gloves, socks and other parts of a soldier's outfit for the army, while the more gifted women were educated to produce traditional Turkish artistic needlework in order to sell it on the market.[66] An Army Sewing Depot was opened in spring 1916 in Gülhane Park in Istanbul. The women employed there sewed army uniforms and in exchange got some money, food and lodging, even if they had a home of their own.[67]

Thus, although they were only a small proportion of the total number of women in need, some women in Istanbul were provided with an opportunity to overcome the financial problems created by the loss of their breadwinner. Women outside Istanbul, however, do not seem to have had such opportunities, except perhaps in the larger towns where there were branches of some of the Istanbul (women's) organizations.

I have tried to show how women in a largely agricultural society were confronted with the effects of the loss of the breadwinner of their family. Unlike women in more industrialized societies such as England and France, where women were able to take the place of men in the workplace, Ottoman women were almost completely dependent on support provided by the state. The state's inability to provide this support adequately, however, left women and their family in a very difficult position. The women in the provincial, rural areas had hardly anywhere to take refuge. Even if they managed to work the fields without any male relatives, the products of their efforts were partly claimed by the state as provision for the army. Women in Istanbul, on the other hand, were somewhat better off: there women's organizations succeeded partly in filling the gap left by the state.

Notes

1   This means that, for example, pensions for widows and orphans, or for those wounded and handicapped in the war, are not dealt with here.

2   Mehmet Zeki Pakalın, *Osmanlı Tarih Deyimleri ve Terimleri Sözlüğü* (3 vols., Istanbul, 1983), vol. 2, p. 573.

3   *Seferberlik Nizamnamesi*, (Istanbul, 1305/1889).

4   So, for example, a man whose father was aged over seventy, or under seventy but unable to earn his living, and who had in his household (*hane*)

neither someone (son, brother, son-in-law, grandson or nephew) who was healthy and over fifteen, nor a son living in another house in the village (*kariye*), would be classed as a soldier on leave (*efrad-ı mezune meyanına idhal olunur*). *Asakir Nizamname-i Şahanenin Suret-i Ahzını mübeyyin Kanunname-i Hümayundur*, (Istanbul, 1302/1886), pp. 14–15.

5   Public Record Office, London, FO 195/2323, no. 116, 26 September 1909.

6   Başbakanlık Osmanlı Arşivi, Istanbul (hereafter, BOA), Dahiliye – Siyasî Kısım (hereafter, DH.SYS), 112-19/35, 26.11.1331.

7   'Hal-i harb münasebetiyle taht-ı silâha celb olunan muinsiz efrad-ı redife ve mustahfıza'nın ailelerine tahsis olunacak maaş hakkında kanun-u muvakkat', *Düstur*, İkinci Tertip, cilt 5, no. 14, 25 Zilhicce 1330/22 Teşrinisani 1328 (5 December 1912), pp. 34–5.

8   'Hal-i harb münasebetiyle taht-ı silâha celb olunan muinsiz efrad-ı redife ve mustahfıza ailelerine tahsis olunacak maaşa müdedair 25 Zilhicce 1330 tarihli kanun-ı muvakkata müzeyyel kanun-ı muvakkat', *Düstur*, İkinci Tertip, cilt 5, no. 34, 24 Sefer 1331/20 Kanunisani 1328 (3 February 1913), p. 53.

9   'Taht-ı silâha alınan muinsiz efrad ailelerine muhassas maaşat için 1329 maliye bütçesine tahsisat-ı fevkalâde olarak 10.000.000 kuruşun sarfı hakkında kanun-u muvakkat', *Düstur*, İkinci Tertip, cilt 5, no. 204, 27 Cemaziyelahir 1331/18 Mayıs 1329 (31 May 1913), p. 510.

10   For instance, at the end of that budget year (1329/1913–14) an extra 10 million kuruş was allocated to the budget. 'Muinsiz efrad aileleri için 1329 maliye bütçesine zamimen 10.000.000 kuruşun sarfı hakkında kanun-ı muvakkat', *Düstur*, İkinci Tertip, cilt 6, no. 167, 14 Rebiyelahir 1332/27 Şubat 1329 (12 March 1914), p. 300.

11   BOA, DH.SYS, 112-19/35, 26.11.1331.

12   *Mükellef iyet-i Askeriye Kanun-u muvakkat*, (Istanbul, 1330/19); *Mükellef iyet-i Askeriye Kanun-u muvakkat*, (Istanbul, 1332/19).

13   *Mükellef iyet* (1330), pp. 19–22; *Mükellefiyet* (1332), pp. 19–22.

14   For example, certain taxes, such as *harç* and *resm*, and the costs of an identity paper to be obtained from the local elder (*muhtar*).

15   *Mükellef iyet* (1330), p. 19; *Mükellefiyet* (1332), p. 19.

16   *Mükellef iyet* (1332), p. 20.

17   BOA, Şura-yı Devlet Harbiye, 662/21.

18   *Mükellef iyet* (1332), p. 21.

19   *Mükellef iyet* (1330), p. 21.

20   *Mükellef iyet* (1330), p. 21; *Mükellefiyet* (1332), p. 21.

21   *Mükellef iyet* (1330), pp. 21–2; *Mükellefiyet* (1332), pp. 21–2.

22   *Mükellef iyet* (1330), p. 22; *Mükellefiyet* (1332), p. 22.

23   For example, Article 55 pointed out that the assigned allowance was to be paid without delay, in the presence of the local committee of elders. They

in turn would receive the money from the agents of the Ministry of Finance (*Maliye tahsildarları*) in exchange for a signed receipt. *Mükellefiyet* (1330), p. 22; *Mükellefiyet* (1332), p. 22.

24 BOA, Şura-yı Devlet Maliye, 480/6.

25 An interesting detail is that, while formerly the term '*aile*' ('family') had been used, this bill specified who was regarded as part of one's *aile*.

26 The bill was not forwarded to the Board of Ministers until August 1918. From there it was sent on to Parliament with the Board's amendments, which softened the strict rules proposed by the Council of State. BOA, Meclis-i Vükela (hereafter, MV), 212/106.

27 BOA, Şura-yı Devlet Maliye, 480/6.

28 BOA, Dahiliye İdare-i Umumiye (hereafter, DH. I-UM), E-29/108, 4C1335; BOA, DH. I-UM, E-30/90, 21C1335.

29 Ahmed Emin [Yalman], *Turkey in the World War* (New Haven, 1930), pp. 147–8, quoted in Zafer Toprak, *İttihat – Terakki ve Devletçilik* (Istanbul, 1995), pp. 142–8.

30 İrfan Orga, *Portrait of a Turkish Family* (2nd edn., London, 1993), pp. 152–76; Cahit Uçuk, *Bir İmperatorluk çökerken* (Istanbul, 1993), pp. 200–49; Hasene Ilgaz, *1915'den 1921'e kadar yatılı bir kız okulun öyküsü* (Istanbul, 1991), pp. 10–11.

31 BOA, Dahiliye Hukuk Müşavirliği (hereafter, DH.HMS), 23/75, 20.4.1331.

32 BOA, Dosya Usulu İradeler Tasnifi (hereafter, DUIT), 50-1/27-4, 30Za1334; BOA, DUIT, 50-1/27-3, 19L1334. On this law see also Toprak, *İttihat*, pp. 135–42.

33 BOA, DUIT, 50-1/27-2, 10C1335.

34 BOA, DUIT, 50-1/27-4, 30Za1334; BOA, DUIT, 50-1/27-3, 19L1334.

35 BOA, DUIT, 50-1/27-1, 3Z1335.

36 BOA, DH.I-UMM, E-25/5, 13S1335.

37 BOA, DH.I-UM, E-11/8, 23Za1333; BOA, DH. I-UM, E-24/42, 29M1335; BOA, MV, 208/100, 18N1335. See also Toprak, *İttihat*, pp. 135–42.

38 BOA, DH.I-UM, E-18/16, 5L1334.

39 'L'Agriculture et les femmes', *İktisadiat Medjmouassi* 2, no. 54 (May 1917), p. 4; 'Die Frau in der Landwirtschaft', *Der neue Orient* 1, no. 7 (July 1917), p. 331.

40 Zafer Toprak, 'Osmanlı Kadınları Çalıştırma Cemiyeti: Kadın Askerler ve Millî Aile', *Tarih ve Toplum* 51 (March 1988), pp. 34–8; Meral Altındal, 'Kadın İşçi Taburu Tarihçesi', *Toplumsal Tarih* 41 (May 1997), pp. 14–16.

41 BOA, MV, 212/69, 7N1336.

42 'Food prices pinch Turks', *New York Times*, 21150 (21 December 1915), p. 3; 'Turks stop meat export', *New York Times*, 21228 (8 March 1916), p. 4 (I am indebted to Yavuz Selim Karakışla for all the quotes from the *New York Times*.) That the food did not always reach the Ottoman soldiers is

clear from Erik Jan Zürcher, 'Between Death and Desertion. The Ottoman Army in World War I', *Turcica* 28 (1996), pp. 235–8.

43 See e.g. BOA, DH.I-UM, E-43/16, 18S1336.

44 BOA, DH. I-UM, 20-2/2-50, 26Ca1336; BOA, DH. I-UM, 20-3/2-30, 26B1336; BOA, DH. I-UM, 20-18/12-1, 16S1336; BOA, DH. I-UM, E-37/49, 1Za1335.

45 BOA, DH. I-UM, E-28/15, 26R1335.

46 BOA, DH I-UM, E-80/35, 9Z1334.

47 BOA, DUIT, 50-1/5-1, 26R1335; BOA, DUIT, 50-1/5-2, 7C1334.

48 BOA, DUIT, 50-1/21-1, 13C1335; BOA, DUIT, 50-1/21-2, 8L1334; BOA, DUIT, 50-1/21-3, 28L1334.

49 BOA, DUIT, 50-1/19-7, 10M1335; BOA, DUIT, 50-1/19-10, 9Za1334; BOA, DUIT, 50-1/19-11, 22N1334; BOA, MV, 207/88, 19C1335.

50 BOA, DH. I-UM, E-34/49, 26Ş1335; BOA, DH. I-UM, E-42/71, 13S1336; BOA, DH. I-UM, E-42/84, 16S1336; BOA, DH. I-UM, E-44/56, 13Ra1336.

51 See, for example, BOA, DH. I-UM, E-30/2, 9C1335; BOA, DH. I-UM, E-30/100, 22C1335; BOA, DH. I-UM, E-32/27, 17B1335.

52 See BOA, DH. I-UM, E-30/106, 23C1335.

53 See BOA, DH. I-UM, 20-2/2-17, 2R1336; BOA, DH. I-UM, 20-2/2-48, 23Ca1336.

54 BOA, DH-UM, 4-1/33, 20Ca1334. Earlier in 1915 food riots and anti-war demonstrations by women had taken place in Istanbul. In order to pacify the angry population, the Ottoman government had to stop exporting meat to Berlin. 'Anti-German riots in Constantinople', *New York Times*, 20928 (13 May 1915), p. 1; 'Riots in Constantinople', *New York Times*, 21079 (11 October 1915), p. 2; 'Food prices pinch Turks', *New York Times*, 21150 (21 December 1915), p. 3; 'Turks stop meat export', *New York Times*, 21228 (8 March 1916), p. 4.

55 Orga, *Portrait of a Turkish Family*, pp. 152–76; Uçuk, *Bir İmperatorluk Çökerken*, pp. 200–49; Ilgaz, *Yatılı bir kız okulunun öyküsü*, pp. 10–11.

56 Kadınlar Dünyası, 'İçtimai: Lady Lowther'e şükran-ı azim', *Kadınlar Dünyası* 1, no. 32, (5 Mayıs 1329/18 May 1913), p. 1.

57 BOA, DH.SYS, 117-7b/7-28, 2.7.1331.

58 Dünyası, 'İçtimai', p. 1; 'Eine Wohltätigkeitslotterie', *Osmanischer Lloyd*, 1913, 31 (5 February), p. 2; *Osmanischer Lloyd*, 1918, 9 (10 January), p. 3.

59 They included the wife of the director of public security, Nuriye Canbolat, the wife of the director of the Printing Office, the wife of Weber Pasha, and the wife of the general director of the police, İrfan Bedri. 'Asker ailelerine elimizden gelen her türlü yardım en büyük vazifemiz', *Tanin*, 2176 (11 Kanunusani 1330/24 January 1915).

60 'Yardımcı hanımlar heyetinin faaliyeti', *Tanin*, 2188 (10 Kanunusani 1330/ 23 January 1915), p. 3; *Galatasarayında Tertib ve Küşad olunan İlk Hilâl-i Ahmer Sergisi Rehberi*, (n.p., 1332), pp. 33–4.

61 BOA, DUIT, 47/1-3, 20C1334; BOA, DUIT, 47/106, 8Ra1336.

62 'Asker Ailelerine Yardımcı Hanımlar Cemiyeti', *Kadınlar Dünyası*, 163, p. 13; 'Asker Ailelerine Yardımcı Hanımlar Cemiyeti', *Vakit*, 122 (29 Şubat 1334/29 February 1918), p. 2; 'Yardımcı Hanımlar Cemiyeti', *Vakit*, 123 (1 Mart 1334/1 March 1918), p. 2.

63 *Devletlü ismetlü Naciye Sultan hazretlerinin zir-i himayelerinde Kadınları Çalıştırma Cemiyet-i İslamiyesi nizamnamesi* (Dersaadet, 1332), p. 2.

64 *Devletlü ismetlü Naciye Sultan hazretlerinin zir-i himayelerinde Kadınları Çalıştırma Cemiyet-i İslamiyesi 1333 senesi raporu* (Istanbul, 1334).

65 Edhem Nejat, 'Türkiye'de kız mektepleri ve terbiyesi', *Türk Kadını*, 11 (17 Teşrinievvel 1334/17 October 1918), pp. 163–5. By 1920, because of mismanagement by three consecutive boards, the society was barely surviving – only 50–60 women were employed at the one branch left. However, the new board seems to have been full of plans for the future, judging by the introduction to a report published in 1920 and dealing with the years 1918–20. *Devletlü ismetlü Naciye Sultan hazretlerinin zir-i himayelerinde Kadınları Çalıştırma Cemiyet-i İslamiyesi 1336 senesi raporu* (Istanbul, 1336/1920).

66 Scheich Abdul Aziz Schauisch, 'Türkische Frauen des roten Halbmondes', *Die islamische Welt*, 5 (1 April 1917), pp. 257–62.

67 Orga, *Portrait of a Turkish Family*, pp. 164–76.

6· Reorganizing Violence: Traditional Recruitment Patterns and Resistance against Conscription in Ottoman Syria

Dick Douwes

In the nineteenth century, in a slow and prolonged process the organization of violence in the 'Syrian' provinces of the Ottoman Empire changed markedly. A highly fragmented system was replaced by a unified system which was open to broader local participation through conscription. The enforcement of conscription was much resented by the subject population, especially because it was preceded by disarmament campaigns in towns and villages. Fear of being left unprotected against violence and of being exposed to it in far-off places inspired many to resist disarmament and conscription. In many areas experience of violence on the part of invading forces, government troops, bands of fugitive cavalry, nomads, landlords, highwaymen or even neighbouring villages and clans had shaped popular conviction that the protection of the community could not be left to the state. The diffused nature of provincial violence and its sometimes intensive use in the decades preceding the reforms meant that these experiences were shared by many. They fitted well into a longer tradition of violence and insecurity. Nevertheless, in the second half of the nineteenth century, after some serious incidents, a provincial regime developed in which the level of violence was unprecedentedly low.

Provincial violence

In the late eighteenth and early nineteenth centuries the 'Syrian' provinces of the Ottoman Empire, in particular Damascus, Sidon and Tripoli, witnessed an, at times, extremely violent rule. In this period the inadequacies of the traditional provincial military regime became apparent. It was a fragmented but fluid system shaped for the collection of taxes and the protection of trade, travel and agriculture. It was not a system qualified for confronting enemy forces. In 1771 the troops of Damascus did not attempt to resist the advance of forces of the Egyptian bey Ali al-Kabir. When Napoleon's troops invaded Palestine in 1789 only the troops of the fortress of Acre resisted, protected as they were by its strong walls. In 1805, provincial troops were unable to preserve the holy cities of Mecca and Medina; to the disgrace of the Sultan the holy sites were ruled for six years by the Wahabi puritans who openly campaigned against Ottoman supremacy.

Local troops seemed better equipped for coercive action against the subject population and for the protection of the main lines of communication. But the trade of the professional soldier in the provinces was insecure, owing to the high degree of competition for local resources and the high demands made by the Porte and its local representatives. The organization of violence prevented the formation of solid, self-contained and enduring forces in the provinces. The incapacity of local rulers to create stable military bases was viewed with some satisfaction in Istanbul. It guaranteed the continuous need by provincial governors for support from the centre, and prevented them from turning their arms against the state centre.

In times of crisis caused by foreign invasions, by natural calamities or by changes in the marketplace, responses to ensuing internal instability were first and foremost coercive. In general, they added to the state of uncertainty because in each and every crisis a part of the military system disintegrated following defeat, disbandment, desertion and irregular payment of troops. Troops resorted to pillage and robbery; only a thin line existed between a highwayman and an out-of-work soldier. Moreover, instability offered the opportunity for contenders to challenge existing provincial authorities. This sometimes resulted in the arrival of non-local troops or, more commonly, in the formation of new local forces with recruits from outside the province, thus damaging the prospects of the local soldiery. In more marginal areas dissatisfied soldiers concluded alliances with local strongmen and sometimes survived for decades under nominal Ottoman rule.

Local and non-local elements in the provincial military

After the occupation of the Syrian provinces by Ottoman troops in 1516 and 1517, the military there had never been entirely non-local. With the conquest of the area, local individuals and groups were integrated into a new ruling class, that of the *askerî*, the soldiers. In the tradition of other empires in the area the Ottoman favoured the employment of non-local troops, but it proved difficult to find a sufficient supply of young men from elsewhere and to prevent locals from joining the Janissaries. In 1577, for instance, the governor of Damascus was ordered to recruit young men from Anatolia instead of locals (*yerli*) and foreigners.[1] The order had no lasting effect and Janissaries continued to be recruited locally. In need of a more loyal military representation, the Porte dispatched fresh Janissaries to Damascus in the mid-seventeenth century; thereafter, the city counted two Janissaries forces: the *yerliyya* and the *qul* (from *kapıkulu*), the commanders of both being appointed by the Porte. This was the situation in some other garrison towns as well, for instance in Jerusalem. In Aleppo, the largest city of the Syrian provinces, the Janissaries remained united, but militia of the local descendants of the Prophet Muhammad played a role similar to that of the *yerliyya*.[2]

In view of the multi-ethnic nature of the empire and the multi-ethnic composition of the Syrian provinces, in particular of the cities of Damascus and Aleppo, the distinction between local and non-local or between indigenous and 'foreign' is not always clear. Local culture was predominantly Arabic in tongue and Muslim in religion, but the Syrian provinces comprised a large minority of Arabic-speaking Christians and small Jewish communities. A clear sense of Arab ancestry existed, at least among literate townsmen, but religious identity was of greater importance in many situations. In the military context religion mattered, because non-Muslims officially did not have the privilege of carrying arms. In practice, many non-Muslims carried arms, particularly in the rural areas, but few Christians or Jews entered the local armies. It is evident from local chronicles that soldiers were normally associated with Kurds, Turkomans, Bagdadis, and Maghrebins (from the Barbary Coast). The last two groups were Arabic-speaking, but clearly of non-local origin. Kurds and Turkomans included locals as well as non-locals, and some may have been familiar with Arabic, but they constituted distinct groups of rural, often nomadic background.

From the use of the Turkish word '*yerliyya*' for local Janissaries one may find some further evidence for the notion that soldiers constituted a 'foreign' institution. The local Janissaries were in many aspects well integrated into Damascene society, but they were of mixed origin. The place of recruitment, rather than the recruits' regional background, seems to have defined their status as *yerliyya*. For instance, some who came as imperial Janissaries (*qul*) later joined the *yerliyya*. Many soldiers from Anatolia or elsewhere who settled in Syrian towns and fortress villages became part of local society, and sometimes married into families of Arab ancestry. The more eminent of them, mostly Kurdish and Turkoman, adopted family names in, perhaps, three generations; a clear sign of integration into the local Arab culture. But they, as well as families of Maghrebin origin, often lived concentrated in certain quarters or villages. The same goes for the local Janissaries; in Damascus they were concentrated in the Midan quarter. A number of these families continued to control military offices well into the nineteenth century.

Local armed groups

Local armed units manifested themselves above all in irregular rural militia, in particular clan-based bands of men from the mountainous and hilly regions. Communities in the coastal mountains and in hilly areas like Nablus in Palestine and Jabal Hawran to the south of Damascus had a marked military tradition and often showed great proficiency. The best-known were the Druzes of Lebanon and the Hawran. They constituted close-knit communities and demonstrated a striking capacity for feuding and fighting. Unlike most other militant communities, Druze chiefs and their men regularly played a role in provincial politics; they transcended the parochial setting in which most other armed clans operated. On occasion they were hired by the Ottoman authorities. In the early seventeenth century the Druze Emir Fakhr al-Din al-Ma'ni and his troops even escorted the *Hadjj* caravan to Mecca. At the time the Porte had no alternative but to engage strong local forces in executing the important tasks of guiding and protecting the pilgrims to the holy places. That Druzes were normally branded heretics or apostates in official declarations was of secondary concern. Much later, on the eve of the introduction of the conscription, Emir Bashir of Lebanon belonged to the more powerful commanders in the Syrian provinces and his mixed Druze–Christian forces to the better motivated and skilled troops.

Other irregular local forces of repute consisted of pastoralist and nomadic groups, in particular Turkomans (migrating between Anatolia and the inland plains of Syria) and *arab*, Arabic-speaking sheep-, camel- or horse-breeders. Like the Druze and other local forces of sedentary background, nomads were regularly contracted by the authorities, but not always as combat units. In particular the highly mobile Beduin received payments to discourage them from using their weapons against caravans – in particular the pilgrimage convoys – and villages in the sown. These nomads protected – or at least were paid to do so – the lines of communication and the fringes of cultivation. With some regularity *arab* forces fought alongside other troops, in particular units of the Mawali tribes which performed police tasks in the open area in between Homs and Aleppo. By the late eighteenth century the systematic employment of Mawali police units in the fringes of the cultivated land had become highly problematic because of the arrival of the powerful Anaza tribes which pushed Mawali and other tribes into more marginal land or into cultivated areas.[3]

Non-local military forces

Local armed bands were mostly clan-based, but local strongmen did not only depend on indigenous combatants. Emir Fakhr al-Din, for instance, recruited mercenary forces referred to as *sakban* (Turkish: Sekban, or dog-keepers). During the unruly first decades of the seventeenth century they constituted the core fighting units, both infantry and cavalry, of local warlords in several areas. Most *sakban* in the Syrian provinces appear to have originated from Anatolia. In the course of the eighteenth century these units lost their prominence, but until the early decades of the nineteenth century *sakban* were employed by, among others, one of the most successful soldiers who served in the Syrian provinces, Jazzar Pasha.[4]

The history of another force of importance, the *lawand* (Turkish: *levend*), followed a pattern similar to that of the *sakban*. Unlike in Anatolia, in Syria *lawand* were not local auxiliaries but mainly Anatolian cavalry, occasionally identified with Kurds. They had the reputation of being proficient soldiers. By the mid-eighteenth century they seem to have disappeared, but the force revived after 1776 when bands of *lawand* from Anatolia were seeking refuge in the Syrian provinces after their official disbanding (see Chapter 1 in this volume). According to a local chronicler, they 'did fear neither death nor ruin'. The French traveller Volney reported that every villager trembled when they passed by.[5] Since their qualities were highly valued, they were hired by several governors, among them Muhammad Pasha (1770–83) of the al-'Azm family of provincial governors. He contracted the commander, Ibrahim Agha Qaysirli, with his following of about 300 horsemen. Jazzar Pasha of Acre engaged other *lawand* groups with the blessing of the Porte.[6]

In the second half of the eighteenth century the most formidable fighting units in the Syrian provinces consisted of *dalatiyya* and the

Maghribins. '*Dalatiyya*' is a corruption of the Turkish word '*deli*', which means 'madman'. These dreaded cavalry units served mostly in the countryside. *Deli*s and their commanders figured prominently in the households of the 'Azm governors and their successors. In Syria *deli*s were closely associated with (Anatolian) Kurds; the Maghrebins were mostly mercenaries from the Maghreb. Mercenaries from North Africa were employed in pre-Ottoman times, but it was only in the eighteenth century that they were recruited on a large scale, in particular in the provinces of Sidon and Damascus. Many of them were sons of professional soldiers of the dey of Algiers who were not enrolled in the dey's army.[7] The powerful Jazzâr Pasha of Acre depended to a considerable extent on these infantry and cavalry forces.

In addition to the non-local forces mentioned so far, Albanian and Bosnian troops, known as *Arna'ut*, operated in the Syrian provinces from the late eighteenth century onwards. Their more permanent presence in the region seems to have been closely connected with the career of Jazzâr Pasha, himself a Bosnian, but the Syrian provinces had witnessed the coming *Arna'ut* forces earlier.[8] After his death their number decreased, but occasionally new parties arrived. In 1808, for example, 500 *Arna'ut* from Egypt landed in Tripoli to support the local strongman, Barbar Agha, in his conflict with the governor of Damascus, the former 'madman' Kunj Yusuf Pasha. Upon their arrival the population of the town escaped to the besieging troops of the pasha.[9] Though the *Arna'ut* were regarded as the most proficient units, they did not replace the *deli*s as the core troops. The *delibashi* (from Turkish: delibaşı head of the madmen) was often the right hand of the governor and a candidate for his successor. *Arna'ut* units remained active in Syria well into the mid-nineteenth century.

Finally, mention should be made of Beduin cavalry units from Egypt, which were introduced into the Syrian provinces in the late eighteenth century. In the wake of the ill-fated invasion by the Egyptian Ali Bey al-Kabir in 1771, about 300 horsemen of the Hawwara tribes arrived in the area in the retinue of his leading military slave Ahmad Bey (the later Jazzâr Pasha). They performed well in local skirmishes in and around Mount Lebanon; in the 1790s their number had increased to, perhaps, as much as 1000 horsemen who were instrumental in extending Jazzâr Pasha's control over Mount Lebanon and the coastal areas. They continued to serve the successors of Jazzâr Pasha, albeit in smaller numbers. Fresh Egyptian Beduin groups entered Syria in 1831 and 1832 in the armies of Mehmed Ali Pasha, who also employed Hinadi Beduin from Egypt. Hinadi tribesmen had come to southern Syria earlier (in 1809), offering their services to the governor of Gaza. When he refused to engage them and ordered them to retreat from his area, the Beduin attacked and defeated his troops, thus demonstrating their proficiency.[10]

Local versus non-local

Apart from a variety of clan-based armed bands, who were auxiliaries at best, and the local Janissaries and militia of Aleppo, in the Syrian provinces the professional and full-time soldiers, as well as their commanders, were mostly of non-local origin. Some of them spoke Arabic, as did the military faction of the Maghrebins. The participation of locals in the regular and mercenary units was low when compared to adjacent Anatolia, and, perhaps, Iraq. By and large, the keeping of order and the use of state violence was associated with Turks, Kurds, Turkoman, Maghrebins, *Arna'ut* and other 'foreigners'. The use of non-locals was systematic and intentional. Governors hardly ever recruited mercenaries from the local population. Even Jazzâr Pasha, who hired every type of soldier one could think of at the time (including Afghans), was reluctant to recruit locally. When he arrived from Egypt in coastal Palestine he started to replace local forces which had served under his predecessor, Ḍahir 'Umar, because they were not to be trusted: 'they were of the same race and therefore of no use in times of need'.[11]

Not all governors and strongmen relied so heavily on non-local forces. Ḍahir 'Umar, who was the principal power in the province of Sidon for over seventy years, relied by and large on his clan and on local troops recruited in and around Galilee. But he and others like him were not Ottomans, in the sense that they did not belong to the class of leading military administrators. Ottoman governors, for instance the 'Azm family and Jazzâr Pasha and his successors from his slave-military household, had a strong local power base, but exercised their power primarily through non-locals.

Fragmentation of the military and increased use of violence

During the eighteenth century the number of military forces active in the Syrian provinces increased; local and imperial Janissary, *sakban*, *lawand*, Mawali and other forces were supplemented by *delis*, Maghrebins, Albanians, Bosnians and Hawwara. The great variety of military forces mirrors the structural fragmentation of the management of violence as well as an increase in the use of violence, particularly toward the close of the century. The provinces of Damascus, Sidon and Tripoli suffered from – at times, extremely – violent rule.

The rule of Jazzâr Pasha can be seen as illustrative of the painful change from pre-modern to modern realities in the Middle East. However, Jazzâr Pasha ('Jazzâr' meaning: 'the butcher') did not pursue modern or even reformist military or economic policies. It is true that he invested great sums in his armies, but he did so by engaging all available traditional military specialists, ranging from Egyptian Beduin to Afghan infantry. Unlike Mehmed Ali Pasha, who arrived in Egypt at the time of Jazzâr's death, he did not implement any military reforms. Jazzâr maintained the distinctive character of the various troops in his service. Only in case of necessity did he combine them. In 1791, for example, his *deli*s, Hawwara, *Arna'ut*, *sakban* and Maghrebin units campaigned jointly in the Shuf area in Lebanon, numbering together with some Druze and other bands, perhaps as many as 12,000 men. The campaign was successful; the local Druzes who followed Emir Bashir were subdued and their emir and his men had to seek refuge in the Hawran to the south of Damascus. Joint expeditions were not always a success; in 1794 Jazzâr Pasha dispatched his *deli*s and Maghrebins to the Matn area in Lebanon and upon arrival they clashed with each other.[12]

Jazzâr's reluctance to use locals for his own troops did not prevent him from seeking the support from clan leaders and their men. In exercising his rule over Lebanon he constantly needed the active support of local armed groups. However rigid and violent his rule was, compared to those of his immediate predecessors and successors, he had no absolute control over his commanders and associates. His increased reliance on excessive violence in his later years accentuated his failure to manage violence in provincial affairs. A suppressed, impoverished and mutilated population – people whose noses and/or ears had been cut off dominated the streets of Acre and Damascus at the time – celebrated his long-awaited death in 1804 and turned against his aides, lynching some and chasing away many others.

The violent character of provincial rule may have been encouraged by external violence; the turn of the nineteenth century was an unruly period in which the region faced a French invasion in Egypt and Palestine and the occupation of Mecca and Medina by Wahabi forces. A few decades later troops of the rebel Mehmed Ali Pasha invaded the Syrian provinces. On all three occasions the military in the Syrian provinces demonstrated a great deficiency in one of the main traditional military duties: defending the realm. The performance of most units was lamentable, not only in the face of better-equipped French and Egyptian troops, but also in the rare encounters with badly armed Wahabi warriors. Negligence of military duties in times of revolt and war was common. The governors, and others like remaining fief-holders, had ceased to contribute to the imperial war effort for over a century. Jazzâr Pasha became the hero of the day when his stronghold, Acre, survived the siege of Napoleon's troops, but earlier he had refused to contribute actively to the war effort. His endurance and that of his former slave-soldier 'Abdallah Pasha during the siege of Acre by Mehmed Ali's troops in 1831–2 could not hide the fact that the military in the Syrian provinces had been shaped to control local tax and trade flows and, at best, to protect sedentary society against nomadic encroachments. Moreover, provincial governors engaged non-local soldiers to protect themselves against the enemy within. These inward-oriented armies were perhaps bound to perform badly in encounters with external forces.

Jazzâr Pasha may be a celebrated case, but he was not unique. A number of professional soldiers both proved themselves in action and also had remarkable careers in provincial government. This was true of all but one of the governors of Damascus between 1785 and 1814. In marked contrast with the preceding period, only one son of a pasha ('Abdallah Pasha al-'Azm) governed the province; the rest were military upstarts. Apart from the soldiers who made it to pasha, a larger group of influential commanders exercised considerable power over longer periods, in particular the commanders of the delis. One such commander, Mulla 'Ismail, survived most of his overlords, including Jazzar Pasha and 'Abdallah Pasha al-'Azm. He was involved in provincial politics and fighting from the early 1780s, when he negotiated a settlement between the governor of Damascus and the rebelling Janissaries, until 1817, when he was killed in a governor's house after having lost his last battle.[13] Some of these professionals had a strong local base, but most were not tied to a specific locality, given their extra-local origin. The delis were strong ethnic military groups, who relied heavily on professional and kinship solidarity on the one hand, and on the great demand for their services on the other. They were used in the Syrian countryside until about 1860.[14]

The geography of violence: peasants and arms

Violence was widespread in Syria in the decades preceding the introduction of conscription, which itself was accompanied by fresh outbreaks of violence. To the great apprehension of many, the actual conscription was preceded by disarmament. Accustomed for centuries to the carrying of arms, many Syrians panicked. They felt profoundly insecure because many communities had experienced clan fighting, theft, robberies, and abuse by regular and irregular troops, and weapons were deemed vital for the protection of quarters and villages and their interests. Other, smaller communities, particularly those in the higher coastal mountains and inland plateaus, had been engaged for decades in highway robbery, particularly in animal theft, and weaponry was one of their main economic assets. To others, the public carrying of arms demonstrated their political or religious – Islamic – prestige.

Opposition to disarmament and conscription was widespread. In some rural areas it took years of military campaigns to disarm villagers and, at the same time, to collect tax arrears. The expeditions regularly ran into serious difficulties, especially in the mountainous and hilly areas of Lebanon, Nablus (in Palestine), and the northern coastal mountains. Rural communities which had a tradition of feuding were often serious opponents. They were well-motivated and proficient. The most feared villagers-in-arms were the Druzes from Jabal Hawran, south of Damascus, the refuge of Druzes who had been on the losing side in clan fighting in Lebanon. They settled in the nomad country of the Hawran in the ruins of villages which had been deserted for ages. Throughout the nineteenth century the Hawran Druzes were the most militant rural group. They were able to evade governmental control to a great extent, even during the firm rule of Mehmed Ali Pasha in the 1830s. Only in the closing decade of the nineteenth century were the first Druzes of the Hawran conscripted for the army.

Another area in which the authorities met with fierce resistance against disarmament and conscription were the Alawite Mountains, the coastal mountains and hills to the north of Lebanon. Like those of the Druzes, Alawite tenets are rooted in Shi'ite Islam and popular mysticism, but the Alawites were considered heretics by most other Muslims. Local chronicles sum up one feud after the other.[15] A number of Alawite clans – then known as Nusayris – competed for the control over valleys and ridges. With some regularity, entire villages were in arms, defending property and life or confronting and, sometimes, taking over neighbouring villages and hamlets. Kinship loyalties were fragmented; in one of the main villages, Qardaha near the coastal town of Latakia, the dominant Kalbiyya clan, for instance, counted five competing subsections which, according to a missionary who lived some years with them, 'have old standing feuds, some of which are kept purposely unsettled, that he who has a claim may keep his antagonist in a state of fear and uncertainty'.[16] A number of neighbouring villages were inhabited by the Bani 'Ali clan. A travelling geographer wrote in his notebook that whenever men from the Bani 'Ali shared their meal with men from the Kalbiyya, they had their riffles at the ready, because once upon a time the Kalbiyya had committed the outrage to attack the Bani 'Ali during supper.[17]

Druzes, Alawites, and the Sunni clans of Jabal Nablus in Palestine, as well as others, did not use their arms only in local conflicts. Many had a reputation for being inclined to rebellion. They often attacked the military convoys who visited their hills and mountains to collect taxes, or to restore order, or to arrest 'masters of decay' – a category which included all sorts of dissenters, ranging from unwilling tax farmers to the brigands who descended from their mountains at night in order to steal cattle, horses and mules in the adjacent plains. Also included were rebellious governors; for instance, in 1821 the Porte accused the governor of the province of Sidon, 'Abdallah Pasha, of making common cause with the Druzes, Shi'ites and Alawites and with Beduin 'culprits'. The various military units present in the provinces often had to face 'dissenters, apostates and rebels against divine rule'.[18]

No reliable figures on casualties are available, but the chance of being killed in local skirmishes was far from negligible. Not only was the peasant population armed, but it also profited from its familiarity with the terrain. Troops were particularly vulnerable in the higher parts of the mountains where they had to go on foot. The terrain of Lebanon and the Alawite Mountains was perfectly suited for ambushes, as well as tactical retreats. Villages were evacuated; provisions were stored in caves; flocks were driven to the heights where troops did not venture to pursue, and, occasionally, houses were dismantled to save the valuable wooden components. On the fringes of the cultivated land both peasants and pastoralists took advantage of the vast and 'empty' quality of their environment, using caves, deserted villages or simply distance as retreats and hide-outs. Precautions could not always be taken and standing crops, trees and terraces were often destroyed by troops. The troops were sometimes supported by local bands: when campaigning in the Alawite region, governors regularly engaged Druze and Maronite forces of Lebanon.

Disarmament and conscription

The Syrian provinces first experienced disarmament and conscription in the 1830s, when they were administered by Ibrahim Pasha, son of Mehmed Ali Pasha of Egypt. His policies in Syria differed from those employed in Egypt and many of them had no lasting effect.[19] During the evacuation of the Syrian provinces by the Egyptian troops, traditional patterns that had been suppressed resurfaced. However, some of the impressions the Egyptians made did last, in particular in the field of the management of violence. First, villagers and townsmen were disarmed; then sons and husbands were taken away to be rearmed elsewhere; they had to fight for alien causes; when, or if, they returned, they were unarmed, exhausted and hungry. When, after the departure of the Egyptians, the Ottomans started to introduce conscription, the population was warned.

Inhabitants of Jabal Hawran, Jabal Nablus and the Alawite Mountains were the first to rebel against Egyptian rule, not because they were loyal to the Ottoman sultan but because the Egyptians had started to disarm them. The Egyptians engaged Druzes and Maronite forces from Lebanon to subdue the protesters. Later they began to collect their arms as well and this 'treachery' sparked off a revolt in Lebanon. Disarmament preceded conscription and, together with the census, these measures encountered fierce resistance. By the use of superior force and drastic measures like burning scores of villages, the Egyptians managed to overcome this opposition, except in the Jabal Hawran. The Ottomans encountered similar resistance when pursuing similar policies in the 1840s and 1850s. Only after heavy fighting in Lebanon in the 1850s, and the massacre of Christians by a Muslim mob in Damascus in 1860, were sufficient means to implement these policies directed to the Syrian provinces.

With the retreat of the Egyptian troops the effects of Egyptian disarmament faded quickly, partly because the Ottomans themselves had distributed arms prior to the arrival of their regular troops. After a decade of Egyptian rule large parts of the population felt relieved; the 'tyrant' had left. The Ottomans were unable to restore the kind of order envisaged in the reforms promulgated in Istanbul during the following twenty years, but according to many in the province traditional order seemed to have been restored. Once again, the management of violence had become fragmented. *Deli*s and other mercenaries resurfaced and numerous clans reoccupied their old positions. When it became apparent to the population that the returning Ottomans were planning disarmament and conscription, objections were expressed in slogans familiar from the Egyptian period. Druze rebels against Ibrahim Pasha in 1840 had stated, 'We shall not give recruits, we shall not pay the poll tax, and we shall keep our arms for ever.' Nearly a decade later rioters in Aleppo shouted, 'We shall not give soldiers, we shall not pay the poll tax.'[20]

It was not until 1845 that the new regular forces, *Nizam*, were positioned in the Syrian provinces and started to collect arms and conscripts. However, owing to limited number of troops available the campaigns progressed very slowly. They were frustrated by frequent reductions in numbers following uprisings in the Balkans and, above all, following the outbreak of the Crimean war; in 1853 nearly the entire regular force of the Syrian province, about 17,000 in number, was transferred to the front. By 1860, on the eve of the massacres in Damascus, the number of regulars had reached at most 10,000. This compared bleakly with the 50,000 to 70,000 regular troops garrisoned in the Syrian provinces during the 1830s by Mehmed Ali Pasha. The *nizam* were supported by the remaining *delis* – now often called *bashibozuks* (Turkish: başbozuk, 'with a broken head') – and a new auxiliary force, the *evniye*, recruited locally. Muslim Arabs, among them Beduin and townsmen, constituted the core of this new force, and a number of them participated in the Damascus massacres of 1860. These events prompted Istanbul to dispatch an additional 20,000 of the best-trained and -equipped troops to the area. Soon after affairs in Damascus had been settled, these troops made their presence felt in many other places.[21]

Escaping from conscription

Strategies to avoid disarmament and conscription in the Syrian provinces appear to have been identical to those followed in other provinces. They ranged from bribing officials to self-mutilation. At first, resistance often was collective and active. In 1852, for instance, regular Ottoman forces were confronted and defeated in a joint effort of Alawite clans.[22] Not only mountain communities but also towns rebelled. In some cases rebellion proved effective: in Aleppo, for instance, no compulsory recruitment of young men for the army occurred until 1861. In other cases, the outcome was the reverse: in

Damascus, mass conscription was among the punitive measures taken after the 1860 revolt had been crushed.

After the events of 1860 collective resistance against subscription subsided. Until the 1880s attempts to conscript youngsters still provoked violent outbreaks in some areas, for instance in the northern, more rugged, parts of the Alawite Mountains and, of course, the Jabal Hawran, where the Druzes resisted conscription until 1896;[23] but in general passive, non-violent and individual strategies became more common. One of the reasons for the passiveness was that it became apparent to many that it was relatively easy to be exempted from service. The ballot system was manipulated, and often those with weak social bonds were selected. Also, the performance of the regular troops improved markedly and, subsequently, discouraged armed resistance. In the wake of punitive expeditions, regular troops levied conscripts as a substitute for the failing ballot system in the Alawite Mountains. Even the most militant of the Alawite clans, like the Kalbiyya and the related Nawasira, became very reluctant to oppose regular units penetrating their mountains after 1870, when several of their leaders had been captured and executed. At the time, these and some other clans handed over 8000 weapons to the authorities, most of them obsolete.[24] However, they continued to attack reserves and units of irregulars whenever those entered the highlands.

Conscription and redefinition of the subject status

Another reason for the waning resistance to conscription may have been adjustment to the changing role of the inhabitants of the Syrian provinces in the Ottoman military system. In the 1860s it became the practice to man Syrian barracks with Syrian soldiers.[25] Although it involved only a tiny portion of the population, the increased participation in the administration, particularly in the keeping of order, was a breach with the past. Gradually, the management of violence ceased to be dominated by 'outsiders'. In time of war, Syrians were dispatched to the front lines to fight for the imperial cause. Of course, most soldiers would rather have remained stationed in Syria, but their participation marked the integrative power of the reformed military trade. The management of violence in the Syrian provinces lost its traditional fragmented and inward-oriented nature, and also became much more effective. Conscription and other military reforms were by and large motivated by developments outside the Syrian provinces, but the reforms created greater discipline in the provinces and, eventually, reduced the actual use of violence to a very considerable degree. Another important aspect of conscription was that it involved religious repositionings. Non-Muslims were exempted from serving; they paid an exemption tax. The loss of predominantly Christian provinces had already increased the proportion of Muslims (as well as Arabs) in the empire. In a sense, Ottoman identity was re-Islamized. This affected the position of heterodox Muslims as well, particularly those who, like the Druzes and Alawites, resisted conscription. There was a need to integrate these communities; increasingly, albeit with great reluctance, officials contemplated the idea that these apostates (according to religious law) had to be accepted as Muslims, or, rather, moulded into correct Muslims. There were also practical reasons; some Druzes and Alawites had the nerve to state that they were not Muslim and, consequently, should be allowed to pay the tax instead of being conscripted. Others converted to Christianity, mainly Protestantism, demanding to be treated as Christians, and some did so in the hope of securing British support. The British and Americans, indeed, showed some sympathy for baptised Druzes and Alawites, but were soon to find out that only very few had embraced Protestantism for reasons of faith.[26]

Apart from the use of force, a number of Ottoman authorities, among them the well-known reformer Midhat Pasha, tried to gain the confidence of the heterodox Muslims by offering them formal representation in local administration. When the status of the Alawites was reconsidered both local Sunni Muslims and Christians expressed their aversion, but for most of the 1870s and 1880s considerable efforts were made to co-opt the Alawite clans. Midhat Pasha, for instance, entertained and lectured their leaders and religious sheiks, an act which would have been considered absurd a few years earlier. The meeting impressed many of those present, as did the attitude of Ziya Bey, governor of Latakia from 1885 to 1892, who tried to win the confidence of Alawites by granting them a full share in local administration and by promoting education among them.[27] Of course, these policies were also motivated by other strategic considerations, especially the wish to curb missionary activities and other foreign interference in the area. However, for some years the Islamization of the Alawites was on the provincial agenda, and a special committee was formed to supervise the building of mosques and schools in their major villages. It was difficult to mobilize the Alawites for this programme; they showed great loyalty their sheiks and saints. Combined with failing funding and the lack of enthusiasm from the part of important sections of Ottoman administration, the measures failed to integrate the Alawites in the Ottoman polity. By the turn of the century most mosques and schools had been converted into stables and storage rooms. Like the Druzes, the Alawites preserved their special identity. As before, a few converted to Christianity, some to Sunni Islam, but they often returned to their original faith later.[28]

The introduction of conscription was part of a complex process which affected the lives of most subjects of the Ottoman sultan, who were faced with unprecedented demands by the central state. In the end the military reforms failed to accomplish their ultimate goal: the survival of the empire. The Ottomans were not able to create a fighting machine which would have enabled them to compete with the British, Russians, and the French. World War I was far from a happy occasion for those who had the duty to fight for the Ottoman cause.[29] Prior to the downfall of the empire, and notwithstanding the outward orientation of the military reforms, the reforms proved more effective in internal than in external affairs. In the last decades of the nineteenth century the population of the Syrian provinces, after strong and often violent protests, profited from a combination of policies centred around the management of violence in the form of a marked reduction in the level of violence. At the same time, the introduction of conscription sparked off a discussion on the relation between religion and (serving) the state in the area. This sensitive discussion was inconclusive, and has remained so.

Notes

1   A.-K. Rafeq, 'Local Forces in Syria in the Seventeenth and Eighteenth Centuries', in V.J. Parry and M.E. Yapp, eds., *War, Technology and Society in the Middle East* (London, 1975), p. 277. On the *yerliyya* of Damascus, see B. Marino, 'Le Faubourg du Midan à Damas à l'époque ottomane: Espace urbain, société et habitat (1742–1830)', DNR thesis, University of Aix–Marseille, 1994.

2   On the military in Aleppo, see H. Bodman, *Political Factions in Aleppo, 1760–1826* (Chapel Hill, NC, 1963).

3   D. Douwes, 'Justice and Oppression: Ottoman Rule in the Province of Damascus and the District of Hama, 1785–1841', PhD thesis, Nijmegen University, 1994, pp. 21–6.

4   Rafeq, 'Local Forces', p. 284; A.-R. Abu Husayn, *Provincial Leaderships in*

Syria, 1575–1650 (Beirut, 1985); Y.J. Nuaysa, ed., *Tarikh Hasan Agha al-Abd* (Damascus, 1979), p. 108; A.H. al-Shihab, *Lubnan fi al-Ahd al-Umara' al-Shihabiyyin*, ed. A. Rustum and F.E. al-Bustani (3 vols., Beirut, 1984), vol. 2, p. 422.

5 M.C.-F. Volney, *Voyage en Egypte et en Syrie dans les années 1783, 1784, et 1785* (2 vols., Paris, 1959), vol. 1, p. 375.

6 Al-Shihab, *Lubnan*, vol. 1, pp. 117–18; A. Cohen, *Palestine in the 18th century* (Jerusalem, 1973), pp. 283–4.

7 Rafeq, 'Local Forces', p. 286.

8 A. al-Budayri, *Hawadith Dimashq al-Yamiyya*, ed. A.I. Abd al-Karim (Cairo, 1959), p. 50.

9 Al-Shihab, *Lubnan*, vol. 2, p. 536.

10 Ibid, p. 544.

11 Cohen, *Palestine*, p. 281.

12 Al-Shihab, *Lubnan*, vol. 1, pp. 166–7, 177.

13 Douwes, 'Justice and Oppression', pp. 74–9.

14 J.H. Skene, *Rambles in the Deserts of Syria* (London, 1864), pp. 64–5.

15 See, for instance, *Athar al-Hiqab fi Ladhiqiyyat al-Arab*, unfinished and undated [prob. 1882] manuscript (private collection, Latakia, Syria); M. Tawil, *Tarikh al-Alawiyin* (Latakia, 1924).

16 Lyde, *Mystery*, p. 210.

17 Hardtmann, *Liwa*, p. 164.

18 Records of the Religious Court (*Mahkama*) of Hama, vol. 48, order dated 30 Ramadan 1237 AH, pp. 314–15.

19 Douwes, 'Justice and Oppression', pp. 127–41.

20 *Mudhakkirat Tarikhiyya an hamlat Ibrahim Pasha ala Suriya*, ed. A.-Gh. Sabanu (Damascus, n.d.); K. al-Ghazzi, *Nahr al-Dhahab fi Tarikh Halab*, ed. M. Fakhuri and Sh. Sha'th (3 vols., Damascus. 1993), vol. 2, p. 375; M. Ma'oz, *Ottoman Reform in Syria and Palestine, 1840–1860* (Oxford 1968), p. 75.

21 Ma'oz, *Ottoman Reform*, pp. 44–60.

22 PRO, Foreign Office, 195/368, n. 10, 7 April 1852.

23 M.L. Gross, 'Ottoman Rule in the Province of Damascus, 1860–1909', PhD thesis, Georgetown University, 1979, p. 43.

24 *Athar al-Hiqab*, vol. 2, pp. 84–7.

25 Gross, 'Ottoman Rule', pp. 74–5.

26 See Balphs, *Fifty Years of Mission Work in Syria* (Latakia, 1913).

27 *Athar al-Hiqab*, vol. 3, pp. 50–52; Tawil, *Tarikh al-Alawiyin*, pp. 454–61.

28 Archives Diplomatiques de Nantes, Correspondance avec les Echelles, Beyrouth, carton 43, n. 7, Latakia, 27 August 1850.

29 Erik Jan Zürcher, 'Between Death and Desertion. The Ottoman Army in World War I', *Turcica* 28 (1996), pp. 235–8.

7· Bosnian Resistance to Conscription in the Nineteenth Century

Odile Moreau

For half a century, Ottoman reformers aimed to impose obligatory military service in the European territories of the empire, but they did not succeed until the second half of the nineteenth century.[1]

The abolition of the Janissary corps outside Istanbul after 1826 met stiff resistance, especially in Bosnia. Here it was more widespread and more violent, and lasted longer (seven years) than in any other province. The reorganization of the army under Sultan Mahmud II and his successors directly affected the privileges and social position of Bosnian military men, who saw the reforms as a double threat: to their class privileges and also to religion through the introduction of westernization. The difficulties encountered by the Ottoman government in the introduction of the reforms in Bosnia stemmed from the political and civic privileges that had been granted to the Bosnian nobility immediately after the Ottoman conquest, in consideration of their religious fervour . At the beginning of the nineteenth century the authority of the Ottoman state in Bosnia was very uncertain. Bosnia was a state within the state, and the Bosnians should be considered more as auxiliaries than as subjects of the empire. To introduce modernizing reforms, it was necessary first to destroy the feudal system. With very few exceptions, Bosnia was divided into as many big and small fiefdoms (known as *sipahilik*) as there were noble families in the country. In practice, these fiefdoms remained the hereditary possession of the families (although in theory Ottoman law severely restricted this system). They were treated as indivisible units and were inherited by all the members of the same family collectively. Under Mahmud II, no new fiefs were granted and the descendants of *sipahis* were gradually trained in schools and progressively integrated the ranks of the new army.[2]

Organisation of a reserve cavalry

The organization of a Bosnian reserve cavalry regiment took place for the first time in 1836; it is first mentioned in an order drafted by a colonel of the reserve (*redif*) cavalry in Bosnia on 13 Şaban 1251/4 November 1835. The order was readily accepted by the population and the regiment was raised in only two months.[3] It consisted of two brigades (*liva*), each of 1000 men; one brigade was located in Bosnia in Zvornik and the other in Klis in Herzegovina. Ultimately, Bosnia provided 10,000 men for service with the reserve.[4]

The raising of the regiment almost coincided with the raising of cavalry regiments in other provinces, such as Erzurum and Kayseri, in 1838,[5] and it probably constituted a test for this kind of refractory province.

There had been widespread unrest, however. In 1831, the Muslim Bosnian landowners and military men led by Hüseyin Kapudan Grascević had come out in open revolt against the Porte. They had demanded autonomy for Bosnia-Herzegovina and the election of a local governor. At the same time they had recognized the sovereignty of the Porte and continued to pay tribute to it. In 1832, after the repression of the revolt, the military officers had been dismissed.[6] The upheaval of 1831 was a forerunner of future troubles. There were also upheavals in 1836, 1837 and 1839.[7]

In 1839, the Edict of Gülhane announced that military service would become obligatory and in 1843 military conscription was introduced for all the Muslims of the empire, though at first only the Turks of Anatolia and Rumelia could be recruited into the regular army.[8] The duration of military service was five years in the regular army (*Nizamiye*) and seven in the reserve (*Redif*). The introduction of conscription provoked such resistance in Bosnia-Herzegovina and İşkodra, however, that the Sublime Porte had to use armed force six times and in the end had to rescind the measure for the Bosnians and Albanians, who in practice were exempted from compulsory military service.[9]

The Reform Decree (*Hatt-i Humayun*) of 1856, which confirmed and expanded the Edict of Gülhane, had no influence whatsoever on the existing situation. Around the end of the 1850s, under the influence of Serbian nationalist propaganda, people in Bosnia-Herzegovina and Montenegro started attempts to free themselves from Ottoman rule. In Bosnia, the rebellions were crushed by the governor of the province, Ömer Lûtfi Pasha (1860–61) and later by his successor, Osman the Lame (1861–9).[10] Very bloody skirmishes went on all through 1860–62.[11]

Military reform in Bosnia-Herzegovina (1864–65)

Serious military reform took place in Bosnia-Herzegovina primarily in the years 1864–5.[12] Two years earlier, the grand vizier and *serasker* (commander-in-chief), Fuad Pasha, had issued a verbal order that local soldiers should be organized in a yeomanry (*mustahfiz*). A military commission met in secret and consulted Bosnian notables.[13] The meeting was presided over by Uzun ('Tall') Abdullah Efendi and seventeen personalities from Bosnia-Herzegovina participated.[14] The object of the meeting was to discuss the introduction of the *Nizamiye* in Bosnia. Many reservations about the reforms were expressed, especially regarding the issue of the soldiers' likely refusal to serve outside the province. In the end the commission had to compromise. It decided that the soldiers would not leave the province.[15]

Another problem was the question of dress – of wearing uniforms, which distracted attention from other, more substantial issues. The Bosnians categorically refused to wear the uniform ordered by the Ottoman Empire. They objected to the new trousers and the hats, which were completely different from native dress. This highlighted the issue of the cultural identity of the Bosnians, and they were authorised to continue to use their own dress for the time being.[16]

A census was ordered for Bosnia-Herzegovina by governor Cevdet Pasha[17] in order to establish enlistment boards.[18] It was decided, taking France as an example, that one Bosnian man in fifty would be recruited for the Ottoman army,[19] under which scheme, 4800 soldiers would be permanently under arms. The conscripts had to perform three years of service, each contingent being renewed by one-third each year. A *redif* served for nine years, and a *mustahfiz* for seven.[20] During the first year the commanders were selected from among the Bosnian Muslims to boost the morale of the troops, but later they were trained at the War College (*Mekteb-i Harbiye*) in Istanbul.[21] Two regiments were formed with six companies and 800 officers. During the first year the first regiment was made up of volunteers because the recruitment papers were not ready yet.[22]

The formation of the regiment was easily accomplished. During the winter of 1864–5, a thousand volunteers enlisted for three years' service in barracks. Volunteers from Herzegovina were called up specifically for the 3rd battalion. The young men from noble families were quickly promoted as officers.[23]

The Bosnian battalions had a fierce appearance and military spirit. Sultan Abdülaziz wanted to see them himself, and had the first battalion of the first regiment brought to Taşkışla barracks in the capital, and then the second as well.[24] In addition to its two regiments of regulars, Bosnia counted 18 *redif* batallions, used to handling arms. In 1874, Bosnia provided a contingent of around 30,000 men, both regular and reserve troops, that had the privilege of serving in the province itself except in wartime.[25]

The end of feudalism

In 1852, Ömer Pasha dispossessed the descendants of the lords, who had converted to Islam after the Ottoman conquest, of their feudal rights: not of landownership but of sovereignty in the territory, which was taken over by the sultan.[26] In the Ottoman Empire, a levy of troops was perceived not as a tax but as a rent on the lord's land. A lord's annual income was fixed in proportion to the size of his landholding. In case of need by the central government, the formerly largely independent feudal lords had to provide the state with the service of an armed and equipped horseman for every 1000 piastres (about 228 francs) annually. One can only make a rough guess of the number of the troops that were provided to the state under this arrangement.[27]

In 1864 a new arrangement between the lords and the government resulted in the reform of the obligatory military service. From now on, this was rendered directly by the Muslim subjects, and not, as previously, by able-bodied men provided and armed by the lords.[28] In 1865, to compensate the lords for giving up these last prerogatives, the pension or annuity recognised by the Ottoman government was granted in hereditary fashion to the eldest son, in accordance with the European order of succession, until the extinction of the family. The holder had to provide service to the state under the conditions mentioned above.[29]

The creation of Timariot Bosnian cavalry regiments.

In 1874 two Bosnian reserve cavalry regiments were created, composed of members of the old feudal families, or *timariots*. They met once a year to receive one month's training. The authorities tried to form the local cavalry as cheaply as possible, and win the loyalty of the great lords to the Ottoman army at the same time. This creation added to the military institutions of the empire a new kind of auxiliary force, a local cavalry.

But the rebellion that broke out in 1875 and the Turkish–Russian wars that followed left little time to prove the value of this institution. The feudal lords were called up only very late, like the irregular troops and the second reserve (*mustahfiz*, or yeomanry), from 1877 onwards. The first call-up was for the Nikshih expedition against Montenegro. Among 20,000 new recruits, there were only a hundred *agha*s (lords) from Mostar, and their zeal left something to be desired. The overall commander (*müşir*), Süleyman Pasha, called the most important together and in an energetic speech, with threatening words, let them know that their service would be soon required.

A French diplomat gave a vivid description of the militia's departure to fight outside Bosnia for the first time.

Your Excellency would have difficulty imagining a more irregularly composed, dressed and armed group of soldiers than the one assembled here yesterday. They were all more than middle-aged, covered in arms of all shapes and sizes and from every age, still wearing the old Turkish dress and mounted on small local horses, which by the way they handle extremely well. They do not seem able to undertake long journeys, or to withstand the privations and dangers of a campaign [but] they left for Mostar...[30]

The *vali* received from Istanbul the order to call up the militia (*asakir-i muavine*, or auxiliary soldiers), which was spread out all over the province, and also the corps of the *sipahi* formed by the old landowning families, about 3600 men.[31] The militia was made up of three classes of the Muslims who had not been called up for service with the regular troops from Bosnia, being either too young, too old or exempted). A French diplomat estimated that about 20,000 men could be raised for active service. This number included a cavalry corps formed by the recently dispossessed lords, which he estimated at 5000 to 6000 men.[32] At the beginning of October 1877, Bosnian 'volunteers' from Bosna-Serai (Sarajevo) and Kagnitz were awaiting in Mostar the departure of the expedition for which they had been summoned. Some 1000 fighters, around a quarter of the horsemen, under separate flags, belonged to the upper class of large landowners. The honorary chief of the expedition was an old man, one of the most respected in Bosnia, the octogenarian Fazıl Pasha, who had to risk his own skin. He took with him his two sons. They were acting at the instigation of the Turks of Mostar and they were incensed by a communication of the Porte containing an expression of the latter's dissatisfaction with their lack of enthusiasm for the defence of their country. Thus challenged, they had decided to leave their own area. Now they found still less zeal among Mostar's local military leaders (ağas), who flatly refused the call to war. Of course, the men who had come to support them told them that if they refused to march, they would themselves go back. A certain number of Mostar's people now joined their ranks, not only becuase they were intimidated but also because they were forced to do so. The military authority collected the Bosnian contingent by force, without granting exemptions to those who brought forward substitutes. But camping out in torrential rain was a hardship to which the local population was unaccustomed, and the Ottomans soon realized that the effectiveness for mountain war of a cavalry corps recruited like that was doubtful. One month later the Bosnian horsemen were indeed sent back home.[33]

Then the feudal troops (sipahis) were ordered to depart for the Serbian front. These troops were badly armed, lacked equipment, had no real military value and could not resist a regular army.[34] All the important lords of the province participated in the campaign. Some were very old and others very young. All these men were followed by horses carrying tents, carpets and all kind of stocks, which would be very cumbersome if and when this troop actually would march into battle. They could be used, however, to guard the borders and so would permit regular troops to be freed to participate in the operations.[35]

The Bosnian cavalry was called up only very late. There was a lack of enthusiasm for rallying to the Ottoman colours in the crisis of 1877. This behaviour seems to contradict the record of the provincial council, which stated that the Bosnian regiments had been raised at the request of interested parties.[36] This declaration is perhaps purely formal and far removed from reality, like the edict of the sultan in 1864 that ordered the organization of two local regiments, explaining that this was in fact at the request of the Bosnians themselves.[37] In fact, in a diplomatic report of 1865, M. Swietochowski, French representative in Mostar, wrote about the intentions of Derviş Pasha, the governor of Bosnia. He wanted to introduce an innovation in the province and sent a circular to the mutasarrıf (governor) of each sancak (district), including Mostar.[38] The aim of this document was to prepare the spirits of the sipahis for their assembly one month every year in every sancak and to promote the creation of a reserve cavalry. The proposition was not approved unanimously and a lot of objections were raised in the meclis (council) of Mostar. For example, it was said that they had never constituted a regular corps, that they had never practised military manoeuvres together and that, if they had to accept these new requirements, they would ask for a total exemption from regular military duty. Hamzi Bey Rizwanbegovič, one of the Mostar *sipahi*s went to Sarajevo with a memorandum of the *meclis* containing these observations. According to the sources, he was very badly received by the governor, Derviş Pasha and when we look at the sixteenth article of the statute (*talimatname*) on the creation of two Bosnian feudal cavalry regiments, we notice that they did not succeed in obtaining exemption from normal military service. The French report seems to establish that the feudal regiments were a new institution created by the Ottoman authorities on their own initiative, and that the *sipahi*s were extremely reluctant to comply. This hypothesis is confirmed by the consular evidence about the behaviour of the *sipahi*s during the Turkish–Russian war of 1877. In fact, at that time there was a notable lack of fighting spirit and the use of threats to mobilise them was deemed necessary.

In spite of these facts, the type of institution created in Bosnia may have served as a model for the Hamidiye cavalry regiments that were created in the early 1890s to protect the eastern borders of the empire with Russia. These were also made up of turbulent parts of the population (Kurdish tribes) whose loyalty the Porte tried to obtain.

Notes

1   For an overview of the structure of Ottoman rule in Bosnia, see A. C. Eren, *Mahmud II zamanında Bosna-Hersek* (Istanbul, 1965), p. 18.
2   See Ömer Lutfi Barkan, 'Timar', in *İslâm Ansiklopedisi* (Istanbul, 1974), vol. 12, p. 331.
3   G. Haberer, p. 100; A.C. Eren, *Mahmud II*, p. 153.
4   H. Kapidzic, 'Die Relation über die Verhältnisse Bosniens und der Herzegowina in mehrfachen Beziehung', in *Prilozi za istoriju Bosnia i Herzegovine u XIX v* (Sarajevo, 1956), p. 42.
5   M. Kütükoğlu, 'Sultan II Mahmud devri yedek ordusu Redif-i Asakir-i Mansure', *Tarih Enstitusu Dergisi* 12 (1981–2), pp. 146–157.
6   *Bosna-Hersek ile ilgili arşiv belgeleri, 1516–1919* (Ankara, 1992), p. 13.
7   H. Sedes, *1875–1976 Bosna Hersek ve Bulgaristan ihtilâlleri ve siysasî olaylar* (Istanbul, 1946), vol. 1, p. 49.
8   E. Z. Karal, *Osmanlı tarihi* (Ankara, 1988), vol. 7, p. 181.
9   *T. T. E. Mec.* 87/10, p. 262-273; Karal, *Osmanlı tarihi*, vol. 8, pp. 354–5, and vol. 7, p. 181; Ahmed Cevdet Pasha, *Ma'ruzât* (Istanbul, n.d.), p. 80.
10 R. Mantran, *Histoire de l'Empire ottoman* (Paris, 1989), p. 511.

136 ARMING THE STATE

11 Sedes, *Bosna Hersek*, p. 51.
12 *Başbakanlık Osmanlı Arşivi* (Ottoman archives of the Prime Minister's office; hereafter BOA), YEE, K.18, E.553/298, Z.93, K.36, p. 1.
13 Ibid, p. 11–12.
14 Ibid.
15 Ibid, p. 19.
16 Ibid, p. 9.
17 Cevdet Pasha (1823–95) was a famous Ottoman statesman and scholar. A religious scholar by training, he was one of the driving forces behind the nineteenth-century reform programme. He is best known as author of a history of the Ottoman Empire in the years 1774–1826. See Christoph Neumann, *Das indirekte Argument* (Münster and Hamburg, 1994).
18 BOA, YEE, K.31, E.27/25, Z.27, K.79.
19 Ibid, p. 3.
20 Ibid, p. 5.
21 Ibid, p. 6.
22 Ibid, p. 15.
23 J. Koetschet, ???, p. 13.
24 Archives Etrangères Nantes (French diplomatic archives in Nantes; hereafter AEN), Turkey, Sarajevo, vol. 18, p. 314, French Consulate in Bosnia, dir. pol. no. 65, Bosna-Serai, 3 September 1865, addressed to the minister of foreign affairs.
25 AEN, Petit Fonds, Sarajevo, no. 4, p. 47, consulate of France in Bosnia, dir. pol. no. 9, dir. co., no. 7, Bosna-Serai, 20 August 20 1874, M. de Vienne to the minister of foreign affairs.
26 AE, CCC, Mostar, vol. 2, p. 225, chancery of the consulate of France in Bosna-Sarai, dir. pol. no. 63, amb. no. 69, dir. cons et aff. co., annex to the dispatch of 13 October 1876, no. 60, M. Wiett. See also AE, CCC., Bosna-Serai, vol. 3, p. 163, dir. des consulats, Juilly, 9 June 1876, E. Chaudty, minister plenipotentiary to M. le duc Decazes. The ministry dates the abolition of fiefs during the year 1851.
27 AE, CCC, Bosna-Serai, vol. 3, p. 327, chancery of the consulate of France in Bosnia, dir. cons. et aff. co., no. 14, Bosna-Serai, 6 September 1876, addressed to M. le duc Decazes, by M. Patin. See also AEN, Petit Fonds, Sarajevo, vol. 4, pp. 44–6, consulate of France in Bosnia, dir. pol. no. 9, dir. co. no. 7, Bosna-Serai, 20 August 1874, M. de Vienne to the minister of foreign affairs.
28 AE, CCC, Bosna-Serai, vol. 2, p. 289, consulate of France in Bosnia, Bosna Serai, 2 February 1874, dir. cons. et aff. co., no. 15, to M. Decazes.
29 AEN, Petit Fonds, Sarajevo, vol. 4, p. 46, consulate of France in Bosnia, dir. pol. no. 9, dir. co. no. 7, Bosna-Serai, 20 August 1874, M. de Vienne to the minister of foreign affairs.
30 AE, CCC, Bosna-Serai, vol. 3, p. 303, consulate of France in Bosnia, dir.

cons. et aff. co., no. 10, Bosna-Serai, August 9, 1877, to M. le duc Decazes, minister of foreign affairs.

31 AE, CCC, Bosna-Serai, vol. 3, p. 379, Consulate of France in Bosnia, dir. cons. et aff. co., no. 25, Bosna-Serai, 30 November 1877, to M. le duc Decazes, minister of foreign affairs.

32 AE, CCC, Bosna-Serai, vol. 3, pp. 32–327, consulate of France in Bosnia dir. cons. et aff. co., no. 14, Bosna-Serai, 6 September 1877, M. Patin to M. le duc Decazes, minister of foreign affairs.

33 AE, CPC, Turquie, Mostar, vol. 3, pp. 122–4, vice-consulate of France in Herzegovina, dir. pol. no. 79, 2 October 1877, M. Dozon to M. le duc Decazes, minister of foreign affairs.

34 AE, CCC, Bosna-Serai, vol. 3, p. 383, consulate of France in Bosnia, dir. cons et aff. co., no. 26, Bosna-Serai, 13 December 1877, to the minister of foreign affairs.

35 AE, CCC, Bosna-Serai, vol. 3, pp. 341–2, consulate of France in Bosnia, dir. cons. et aff. co., no. 15, Bosna-Serai, 13 September 1877. The sultan telegraphed that the Bosnian army's privileges were suppressed. Some battalions should leave the province to go to Sofia. Cf. AE, CCC, Bosna-Serai, vol. 3, p. 370, consulate of France in Bosnia, dir. cons. et aff. co., no. 12, 21 September 1877, M. Wiet to M. Waddington, minister of foreign affairs. The abolition of the landlords' privileges was ordered in 1878. Cf. AE, CCC, Mostar, vol. 1, p. 92, vice-consulate of France in Mostar, dir. cons.

36 BOA, YEE, K.18, E.553/85, Z.93, a.

37 AEN, Petit Fonds, Sarajevo, vol. 2, pp. 8–9, dir. pol. no. 65, Bosna-Serai, 3 September 1865, to the minister of foreign affairs.

38 AEN, Petit Fonds, Sarajevo, vol. 19, chancery of consulate of France in Herzegovina, Mostar, 23 October 1874, J. Swietochowski to M. de Vienne, who was in charge of the vice-consulate at time.

8· The Revolts of 1916 in Russian Central Asia

Sergei Kudryashev

The revolts against the recruitment drive for labour battalions in the tsarist army, which occurred in 1916 in the Russian possessions in Central Asia, have been treated in a number of distinct ways in Soviet and post-Soviet historiography. Early Soviet historiography emphasized the revolutionary character of the revolts against tsarist oppression, which it depicted as a kind of forerunner of the revolution. In the Stalinist and post-Stalinist eras, and certainly with the resurgence of Russian nationalism during World War II, Russian rule in Central Asia was reinterpreted as bringing progress to the backward, 'feudal' areas of Central Asia and, accordingly, the revolts were described as reactionary movements. In the post-Soviet era, of course, the rebels of 1916 are generally seen as precursors of the nationalists of today in the newly independent states of Central Asia. A dispassionate look at the events of 1916 is needed to de-mythologize their history.

The territory where the events took place in 1916 was known in the Russian Empire as Turkestan ('the country of Turks'). It consisted of five huge regions and two autonomous khanates (Khiva and Bukhara) with a total population of around 10 million people, of whom about a million were Russians.[1] The social unrest in this area, which in some cases developed into open military confrontation, was a part of the general crisis of the empire during World War I. Russian participation in the war sharply increased the demand for human and natural resources. To ease the burden, the tsarist government took a decision to exploit its Central Asian possessions.

Under the Russian system of conscription in force at the beginning of the century, the non-Slavs of the empire were never conscripted. Though this question had been discussed for years in government circles, no definite decision was made before World War I. But when in

1915 the total number of Russian losses (dead, wounded, missing and captive) approached the frightening figure of 3.5 million,[2] the Russian War Ministry sent the tsar a draft of a new order to conscript non-Russians and non-Slavs for service in the army. At first Nicholas II did not approve of the idea and recommended a thorough study of the possible outcome. The main reason was that the non-Slavs were regarded by many in the general staff as inferior to the Russians. The inhabitants of Turkestan did not know the Russian language and had no military training. Some officers stressed the unreliable character of Turkestan's peoples, others called them rubbish.[3] For all these disparaging attitudes, it has to be said that many non-Slavs considered their right not to be recruited for military service a very important privilege. Once they had acknowledged the supreme power of the Russian tsar, they were exempted from some duties which the indigenous population had to shoulder.[4]

Having temporarily postponed the problem of conscription of non-Slavs, on 1 August 1915 the central government introduced a special military tax which was to be collected from all non-Russian populations, including the Muslim population of Turkestan. But soon this measure proved insufficient. The money collected did not provide more soldiers, and the problem of human resources was getting more and more acute. As a result, the government again turned to the human potential of the Central Asian possessions. Three times (3 May, 6 May and 14 June 1916) the Council of Ministers discussed the matter, and eventually it found a 'solution'. In order to free trained Russian soldiers from duties in the rear and send them to the front line, the Council decided to replace them by conscripted non-Slavs from the 'colonies'. On 25 June 1916 the tsar signed an order, 'On conscription of the non-Slav population for the rear service of the active army', which imposed conscription on the male population between the ages of nineteen and forty-three; later, the upper age limit was reduced to thirty. The government planned to recruit around 400,000 people, 250,000 of them from Turkestan.[5]

The government realized all the difficulties involved in this operation and did its best to explain the necessity of the action. But in spite of central propaganda the immediate response of the local population was unanimously negative. The first days of drawing up lists of future conscripts caused social unrest which, in some places, turned into real revolts. In one small town, Khojand, an angry crowd gathered outside the building of the local administration. They demanded a halt to the drawing up of lists of conscripts. Receiving no answer, some peasants began to throw stones through the windows. The small garrison responded with their weapons. After the first shots the crowd dispersed, and by 3 p.m. life in the town had returned to normal. Two peasants were killed, thirty wounded and forty arrested.[6] From this incident of 4 July many Soviet historians date the 'beginning of revolt' in Central Asia.

Obviously, one should not exaggerate the revolutionary impact of Khojand. One can hardly regard it a revolt, since it lasted for only three to four hours, no damage was inflicted on the local authorities, and order was restored easily and swiftly. Similar cases took place everywhere throughout the country. What was far more important was the psychological effect. Without radio and television people relied on rumours. These quickly spread around the region, and soon many spoke about thousands dead and few believed that the rebels had lost. The fact of the open protest in Khojand acquired a symbolic meaning, and the same scenario was repeated in many places. As a rule, furious peasants tried to catch officials responsible for drawing up the lists of conscripts, beat them and destroy the lists. According to government sources there were 131 open protests in all. But this figure conflicts with those in police files, and there were many more cases of officials being attacked and even murdered.[7]

July 1916 proved to be the hardest time for the tsarist administrators in Turkestan. All kinds of disturbances happened everywhere, but police forces were limited. In the whole of Turkestan, the authorities had approximately 80,000 troops and 10,000 policemen at their disposal. They could also rely on so-called detachments of self-defence recruited from Russian settlers in the region. These well-equipped detachments were organized specifically to deal with cases of social agitation and emergencies. Hostility towards Russian colonizers resulted in a few places in massacres of the Russians, for example in the Djizak region (now in the territory of Uzbekistan), where local nationalists declared *gazavat* ('holy war') and killed 113 Russians. The Djizak revolt was brutally suppressed by the army. Several villages were completely destroyed, the central part of the town was set alight and a part of the local land was confiscated.[8] The executions in Djizak frightened the regional population to such an extent that no serious protests were recorded after 25 July 1916.

The revolt which received most publicity was that in Kazakhstan headed by Amangeldy Imanov, a talented warlord, who managed to create a relatively disciplined Kazakh army. Imanov divided his forces into mobile detachments and arranged good communications between them.

He also built several workshops which produced primitive, but effective, weapons. Having realized the danger of the organised rebel forces, which reached a peak strength of about 50,000 in November, the central government sent the whole division of General A. Lavrentiev to fight against Imanov. The high-water mark of the revolt came in October–November when, for nearly three weeks, Imanov's forces tried to take the town of Turgai. Despite their superiority in numbers the rebels could not defeat the small, but well-trained and well-armed town garrison. The arrival of Lavrentiev's division and the consequent failure at Turgai forced Imanov to change to guerrilla warfare. Russian troops chased the rebels, caught and killed many of them, but did not manage to arrest Imanov, who, with a small part of his forces, escaped to remote lands in the north. From there he still harrassed the government but was not able to interfere with the conscription.[9]

All major centres of resistance in Turkestan had already been suppressed during July–September 1916, mostly by the use of military force. Experienced, mobile, well-equipped Cossack detachments literally crushed numerically strong, but badly organized and poorly armed crowds of Muslim peasants. There were a few cases of Russian soldiers refusing to shoot unarmed people, but those were the exception. Military reports often mention huge losses by the rebels and very rarely say anything about losses on the government side. In addition, special punitive expeditions were sent to restore order, the result often being the looting of the population.[10]

Lack of experience, of good administration and of any reasonable programme doomed the rebels to failure. Meanwhile, one must render the tsarist government its due. Many of its actions were slow, but rather effective. On 17 July martial law was introduced in Turkestan. Meetings and anti-government propaganda were prohibited. The central administration took into account the interests of the Central Asian nobility and the rich. On 23 August 1916 the conscription law was altered in favour of the latter. Special categories of the non-Slav population, notably clerics, policemen, students, government employees and the nobility, were exempted from military service. The definition of these categories met the expectations of the upper classes in Turkestan and turned round the situation with regard to conscription. Moreover, and this was extremely important, the new law allowed people to pay an exemption fee. It also made it possible to find a person of the same nationality, pay him and send him as a substitute for 'service in the rear'. This option was open only to the well-to-do: it normally cost about 1000 rubles, at a time when a skilled worker could expect to earn 45–50 rubles per month. These measures undoubtedly helped the government to pursue its policy. It did not manage to conscript the desired figure of 250,000 but 123,000 Uzbeks, Tajiks, Turkmens and Kazakhs were taken into the army for garrison duties in September–November 1916. Did the end justify the means? The total losses and gains still have to be counted. The government's military losses are not clear, but they could hardly exceed 500 dead. As for the civil population, it suffered tremendously. Approximately 350,000 people had to leave their homes. Some tried to escape to China and Persia, and many perished on the way. Officially, 3000 people were punished in Turkestan 'after the events', but the real number is probably twenty times as high. Had the government invested its money and resources in the raising of troops in exchange for direct payment, it might have raised many more troops than it did through the introduction of a conscription system.[11]

Notes

1   See P.P. Semionov, *Geographico-statisticheskiy slovar Rossiyskoi imperiy* (St Petersburg, 1885), vol. 5.

2   *The First World War in Figures* (Moscow, 1934).

3   S. Ubaidullayev, *Na zare revolutsiy* (Tashkent, 1967), pp. 84–5; B. Suleimenov and V. Yasin, *Vosstaniye 1916 goda v Kazakhstane* (Alma Ata, 1977), p. 73.

4   Suleimenov and Yasin, *Vosstaniye*, pp. 73–4.

5   Ubaidullayev, *Na zare revolutsiy*, pp. 85–7; *History of the USSR*, vol. 6 (Moscow, 1968), pp. 618–19; *Vosstaniye 1916 goda v srednei Azii i Kazakhstane* (Moscow, 1960).

6   H.T. Tursunov, *Vosstaniye 1916 goda v srednei Azii i Kazakhstane* (Tashkent, 1962), pp. 3–17; Ubaidullayev, *Na zare revolutsiy*, pp. 89–95.

7   *History of the USSR*, p. 620; State Archive of the Russian Federation, Collection of the Police Department, Subdepartment 4, 1916, file 130, part I, vols. 1–5; part II, vols. 1–2.

8   Z.D. Kastelskaya, *Osnovnye predposylky vosstania 1916 goda v Uzbekistane* (Moscow, 1972), pp. 115–19; Ubaidullaev, *Na zare revolutsiy*, pp. 99–100; Russian State Military Archives, Turkestan Military Region, Collection 1396, Correspondence, index 4, file 206, pp. 1–24.

9   Suleimenov and Yasin, *Vosstaniye 1916 goda v Kazakhstane*, pp. 108–13; *History of the USSR*, p. 620; G. Sapargiev, *Karatelnaya politika tsarisma v Kazakhstane* (Alma Ata, 1966), p. 305; RSMNHA, Collection 1720, index 15, file 658, pp. 53–5; State Historical Archives (St Petersburg),

Collection 1291, index 82, file 1933, pp. 446–7. Imanov continued his struggle even after the February 1917 revolution in Russia. Later he supported the Bolsheviks and helped to create soviets in Central Asia. He was killed by anti-Soviet forces in May 1919.

10 State Archives of the Russian Federation, Collection of the Police Department, Reports on Asia, file 130, part X, pp. 1–185; file 365, pp. 46–7, 299–309; RSMHA, Archives of the General Staff, Collection 400, index 1, file 4524, pp. 1–93.

11 Ubaidullayev, *Na zare revolutsiy*, pp. 114–16; K. Usenbayev, *Vosstaniye 1916 goda v Kirgizii* (Frunze, 1967), pp. 232–43.

9· Conscription and Popular Resistance in Iran, 1925–1941

Stephanie Cronin

For the nationalist regimes of the inter-war Middle East, Riza Shah's Iran, Mustafa Kemal's Turkey and Hashimite Iraq, the construction of a strong national army based on universal military service was an essential element of state-building and nation-formation. Although conscription was ardently advocated by the nationalist intelligentsia, wherever it was actually imposed it aroused intense resentment and was almost universally unpopular. Yet mass, collective and organized resistance was comparatively rare. In Iran such resistance occurred in three waves in the late 1920s. Uniquely in the Middle East, opposition in Iran was most sustained not in the rural areas but in the towns, in Isfahan and Shiraz in 1927 and in Tabriz in 1928, where it was led by the guilds and the ulama, although violent opposition was also manifested by the tribes in 1929. Riza Shah was irrevocably committed to conscription, which was a central pillar of his programme of modernization and secularization, and, although prepared to temporize, was ultimately determined to crush collective resistance. By 1930 he had largely succeeded in so doing. The subsequent implementation of the policy was aided by a deliberate decision to defuse popular anger by tolerating, even encouraging, individual strategies of avoidance, in particular by allowing the manipulation of the exemptions system through bribery. As the 1930s progressed, conscription became established as an indelible feature of the new Iran.

The Bunichah system

In Iran modern conscription was first systematically enforced by Riza Shah in the second half of the 1920s, yet the measure itself, and its centrality to programmes of defensive modernization, has a much older pedigree. The first attempt to impose conscription was made in the early nineteenth century by the crown prince, Abbas Mirza. Directly inspired by the Ottoman example, Abbas Mirza devised a rudimentary scheme, known as the *bunichah* system, which he introduced in Azarbayjan as part of his attempts to construct a modern standing army with which to confront the Russian advance southwards.

The *bunichah* system was taken up by Amir-i Kabir, the reforming prime minister of the new shah, Nasir al-Din, and incorporated into his efforts to create a standing army as part of an overall reform of the state and government between 1848 and 1851. Although, like Abbas Mirza's experiment, Amir-i Kabir's wider programme ended in frustration, he did preside over the introduction of the first generalized and country-wide, albeit still rather primitive, system of conscription in Iran, a system which was to endure down to 1925.[1]

Under Amir-i Kabir the *bunichah* system was developed into a relatively complex measure. In the absence of more general administrative reforms, most importantly a census, responsibility for furnishing recruits was fixed collectively on the village, not on the individual. Liability for military service was tied to revenue assess-ments in the countryside. The method of calculation was to carry out a survey of the number of ploughs required to keep an area under cultivation, and to reckon on one man per plough as available for military service.[2]

From the early 1850s, then, an approximation of a modern, stand-ing army based on a form of conscription existed in Iran. However these *nizam* regiments were, from a military point of view, almost completely useless. In practice, the shah and his government still relied, as they had before any reforms were carried out, on irregular cavalry drawn from the tribes. These tribal levies, the men serving under their own chiefs and called into the field only for specific campaigns, constituted the only fighting force of any real effective-ness possessed by Iran throughout the nineteenth century, and they continued to be an important element of the army's fighting strength well into the twentieth century.[3]

The *nizam* in Iran played no role comparable to that of the reformed army in the Ottoman Empire. It was marginal to the political and military history of the period, which included the constitutional revolution, World War I and the coup of 1921, and was not able to comprise a nucleus for the revitalized army of the 1920s.

That role fell rather to the two semi-modern forces created independently of the *nizam*, the Cossack Brigade/Division and the Government Gendarmerie, both of which depended largely for their rank and file on voluntary recruiting from the tribes.[4]

The reforms of Riza Pahlevi

In 1921 Colonel Riza Khan, using the Iranian Cossack Division, carried out a coup which inaugurated a new period both in the general political history of Iran and also, specifically, in its military development. First as war minister, then from 1923 as prime minister also, and from 1926 as shah, he embarked on the project of building a modern, centralized state, anchored in the ideology of secular nationalism, at the heart of which would be a modern army.[5]

Immediately after Riza Khan's coup, what remained of the *nizam* was incorporated into the Gendarmerie, which was then itself merged with the Cossack Division.[6] These were to be the foundations of the new army. Plans were laid for rapid military expansion, including intensive enlistment, although no new recruiting policy was yet in place. In fact, in the early 1920s the army continued its reliance on the *bunichah* system, supplemented by voluntary enlistment and the permanent incorporation of small tribal contingents. However, the bulk of the actual fighting of the many campaigns of these years was still done not by the regular troops but by the irregular tribal levies, raised and disbanded as occasion required.

The defects of the *bunichah* system had been generally recognized since the nineteenth century. A disadvantage of particular and increasing seriousness for a modern army was that it was imposed only on the agricultural districts, which could ill afford to spare labour, and did not apply to the towns, where there was a pool of underemployed manpower and where skilled and better-educated labour might be found for the technical services. Furthermore, although theoretically applicable to the whole country, with certain exceptions the system was in fact only very partially enforced, imposed on parts of the country which had been traditional recruiting grounds, mainly Azarbayjan, and leaving other districts, notably the south, entirely exempt. The legal exceptions were significant and numerous: the inhabitants of towns where the land tax was not levied; *sayyid*s (descendants of the Prophet); the ulama; peasant cultivators of the crown lands; and all non-Muslims – Christians, Jews and Zoroastrians. Another serious problem was that no new revenue assessment had been made since the original survey of the early 1850s. Fluctuations in population meant that quotas were out-of-date and anomalous. When a recruit was taken, the length of service was for life unless the soldier could buy a discharge from his superior, and the *bunichah* system was inevitably intensely unpopular with the peasantry, led to the recruitment of the 'village failures' and provided ample scope for bribery and corruption.[7]

In the early 1920s the army made the first serious attempt to enforce the *bunichah* system throughout the country. However, the out-of-date quotas and the system's application to areas which, although theoretically liable, had customarily been absolved, led to turmoil in the countryside. In September 1923 it was reported from Kirman, hitherto always exempt, that forcible enlistment was causing panic in some villages and constituted a rich source of bribes to recruiting officers.[8] Indeed the situation became so bad that by October the commanding officer had halted recruiting, owing to the general uproar in the district over extortion by recruiting officers. Some villages had already been entirely deserted. A year later the situation in Kirman had not improved. According to the British consul, both the army and military service had continued to grow in unpopularity, resulting in an increasing difficulty in obtaining recruits in the province. Landowners were being harried by the military authorities to provide recruits and were being obliged to pay their tenants larger and larger sums to induce them to enlist. On 21 August 1924 a group of these landowners threatened to take *bast* (sanctuary) in the British consulate in protest against the pressure being brought to bear on them by the army.[9]

During the years 1922–6 numerical growth was slow and difficult and the provincial divisions remained considerably below their targeted strength of 10,000 men each. By the beginning of 1925, the army still numbered less than 50,000. Riza Khan had quickly become exasperated with the army's antiquated recruiting methods, and between 1923 and 1925 forced a conscription bill through the Majlis. He was supported in this by the nationalist intellectuals of the Revival and Socialist parties. For this trend, represented by the veteran constitutionalist Hasan Taqizadah, the construction of an army based on conscription was an essential step both in the achievement and defence of national sovereignty and in the creation and inculcation of national identity. Religious opposition having been neutralized by a concession granting total exemption to all religious students, the conscription bill was passed by the Majlis in June 1925.[10]

Although exemption had been granted to religious students, no concession was made to traditional Muslim sentiment regarding the application of conscription to the Christian, Jewish and Zoroastrian minorities of Iran. When the deputy Sayyid Hasan Mudarris stated during the debate in the Majlis that, although bearing arms was a religious duty of the Muslim, non-Muslims were under no obligation and should not be compelled to serve in the army, a Zoroastrian deputy, Arbab Kaykhusraw, made a spirited defence of his community's right and desire to share equally in the burdens as well as the privileges of citizenship.[11] Although in practice there was already a significant Armenian presence in the army, in the form of an independently organized squadron with its own officers, the government's insistence on the general participation of the non-Muslim minorities, and the public and official recognition of this participation, represented a complete break with the past and symbolized the triumph of nationalism over religious and communal identity. However, the enthusiasm of sophisticated, politically conscious urban leaders was not altogether shared by the peasant constituencies. In January 1925, for example, the Christians of Urumiyah district were reported to be much disturbed by the government's intention to impose conscription on them and to have decided to emigrate if this were indeed the case.[12]

Although the conscription act contains references to the legitimacy of conscription in terms of Islamic law, its ideological inspiration was clearly that of modern nationalism. In a preamble the act outlined the defects of the *bunichah* system and the benefits to be derived from a system of universal military service. It was stated that conscription would give the Iranian army a national character and would give all families in the country an interest in defending their nation and their independence. The army would be made strong enough to ward off any attack, taxation and recruitment would be fairer, ensuring that enough persons remained to cultivate the land, and economies could be effected in the pay of the army. Point 7 of the preamble declared that conscription would result in an increase of patriotic sentiments among the Iranian people, mutual good feeling between various classes and the creation of feelings of equality, while point 8 stressed the virtues of the avoidance of discrimination and the equality of all before the law.

The act imposed liability for military service on all males on reaching the age of twenty-one, with certain exceptions, of which the most important were clerics and religious teachers, religious students and certain defined categories of men on whom others were dependent. The period of service was twenty-five years, divided into three categories: six years' active service, of which two were to be spent with the colours and the remainder in immediate reserve; thirteen years' reserve service; and six years' service in the local guard (only to be called out in time of war). Reservists were to come up for training each year for varying periods. The men taken for service with the colours in any one year were to be chosen by the drawing of lots from among those liable for military service.

After the passage of the act through the Majlis, the government began to make various preparations for its implementation. The Ministry of War could not begin to conscript recruits until the Ministry of the Interior had completed the national census, work on which had started earlier in 1925. By the end of the year recruiting officers were being trained in their duties at Tehran prior to being sent to the provinces, where they were to assist the officials of the Interior Ministry in taking the census and subsequently to begin enlisting conscripts. During early 1926 preparatory work for the enforcement of conscription progressed extremely slowly. It was not until the end of October that Riza Shah signed a decree ordering the application of the act from 7 November. Early in November notices were duly published warning all men in Tehran born in 1905 that they should present themselves to the recruiting commission on certain dates, according to the districts in which they lived, beginning with 7 November. The penalty for failing to appear was forcible enlistment and service for three years instead of two. Those entitled to exemption were requested to bring with them certificates from the relevant authorities.

The recruiting commission completed its work in Tehran towards the end of November but the results fell considerably short of expectations. Of the 1486 drawn by lot, 1160 had failed to present themselves, while the remaining 326 were taken into service. The absentees either had absconded or did not exist, fictitious names having been entered on the census register by persons wishing to obtain extra voting-cards for the Majlis elections.[13]

The Ministry of War had begun to apply the conscription law in Tehran and its environs, where government control was more complete and the army more reliable, as it had immediately become apparent that considerable popular opposition to the measure existed throughout the country. In Kirman, for example, the announcement of the ratification of the law had been received with open apprehension, while the initial work of the recruiting commission in Tehran in early November had produced hostile demonstrations. Rumours were gaining currency within the army itself that the ulama of the Shi'ite shrine cities of Najaf and Karbala had pronounced against conscription and that the measure was British-inspired.

By the end of 1926 the imposition of conscription was still limited almost entirely to the capital and its environs, the provinces of Tehran, Qazvin and Hamadan, and even there had yielded disappointing results. Exemptions were numerous and the number of men conscripted did not exceed 2000–3000. In early 1927 the government formulated the clear intention to apply the law more energetically throughout the country. Recruiting offices were established and calling-up notices posted in all the provincial capitals. Strong opposition immediately appeared. For example, in January disturbances broke out in Sultanabad following the arrival of recruiting officers. The bazaars were closed and the offices of the recruiting commission attacked. These disorders were only quelled by the arrival of more troops.[14] Nevertheless the government pressed on, although it quickly became impossible for it to ignore the fact that recruitment was being accompanied by gross corruption. In May a joint commission, consisting of representatives of the Ministry of War and the Ministry of the Interior, left Tehran to tour the provinces to inquire into the complaints made regarding the methods used in the enforcement of conscription.

Although resentment at conscription was intense, it had so far resulted only in sporadic and spontaneous defiance. However, the attempt to impose conscription on the towns of southern Iran in the autumn of 1927 produced a dramatic, concerted and well-organized example of popular resistance. Prior to 1921 the agriculturally based *bunichah* system had customarily not been enforced in the south, and the army's efforts in the early 1920s to take recruits from the peasantry in Fars and Kirman had been met with shock and hostility. The unprecedented imposition of conscription on the towns of the south was intolerable to the urban population, and the labour guilds in particular were solidly opposed to the new law.

Anti-conscription protest

The anti-conscription movement in southern Iran was led by the ulama, who utilized to the full their traditional networks of support among the guilds and the merchants in the bazaars. During the passage of the conscription bill through the Majlis clerical deputies had put up little opposition, yet the underlying concern of the ulama at the secularizing impact of military service was apparent. By 1927 for the ulama conscription had become enmeshed in a web of hostility to the central government and the shah.[15] In his rise to power Riza had always retreated when faced with concerted religious opposition, most famously in his abandonment of republicanism in 1924, and had been careful to compromise at certain key moments. But in 1927–8, following the stabilization of his newly founded dynasty, his regime introduced a raft of radical secularizing, centralizing reforms, and began their implementation in an aggressive manner. The ulama were aware that the balance of power between themselves and the regime was about to alter decisively to their detriment. Although on the defensive, they were bracing themselves for a struggle. They were particularly angry at the reorganization and secularization of Iran's judicial system, which was pushed through during 1927 and which threatened their role, status and income, indeed deprived altogether large numbers of minor clerics of their livelihoods. Another momentous change heralding rapid and profound cultural secularization and enforced uniformity was inaugurated by the cabinet's decision in early August to make the 'Pahlavi hat', similar to the French kepi, the official headgear for Iranian men.[16] The ulama were also anxious and fearful at the rise of Abd al-Husayn Taymurtash, the shah's new minister of court and a strong advocate of modernization, who they believed had influenced the shah against them. They had been especially provoked by the formation in August 1927, by Taymurtash and other leading secularizers, of the New Iran party, from membership of which anyone not wearing the Pahlavi hat was expressly debarred, a provision aimed at the turban-wearing ulama. They also gave free expression to the cynicism and anger widely felt by the general population at the conduct of elections to the sixth Majlis, which had been rigged by the authorities.

The increasing friction between regime and ulama gave rise to a number of incidents during 1927. Between 16 and 25 April the bazaars in Shiraz were closed, there were mass demonstrations with some rioting, and telegrams were sent to leading *mujtahid*s and the Majlis, over the deportation by the military authorities of a minor mullah who had denounced the registration of women for the census. The military authorities were forced to yield and permit the return of the deported mullah.[17] In late August the ulama of Isfahan led demonstrations of protest at the arrest of a preacher who had criticized the shah and the introduction of the Pahlavi hat. For eight days the Isfahan bazaars were closed, and crowds assembled at the telegraph office to send telegrams to Tehran. The preacher was accordingly released and the ulama went on to demand successfully the dismissal of the chief of police.[18] In October the ulama in Tehran, Isfahan and Mashhad launched a campaign against the New Iran party. Leading clerics in Tehran threatened to leave the city, and those in Isfahan threatened to go into *bast* in Qum. Thereupon the shah, in any case exasperated by the squabbling to which the party had been prone, advised it to cease its activities.

As these skirmishes indicated, the ulama were still capable of achieving limited victories at the local level. However, their capacity to oppose the regime over a major issue was severely hampered by the lack of an outstanding figure who could offer national leadership. In the capital itself, to which the provincial ulama increasingly looked, the few important *mujtahid*s were highly vulnerable to pressure from the central government. The centre of gravity of the movement against conscription therefore shifted to southern Iran where opposition was fiercest.

Isfahan took the lead, followed by Shiraz and by towns in other regions including Tehran, Mashhad and Qazvin, although Isfahan and Shiraz in the south became and remained the centres of the anti-conscription movement. The protest began when the aged *mujtahid* Ayatullah Haj Agha Nurullah Isfahani, in response to a request from the people of Isfahan, agreed to go to the shrine city of Qum[19] and from there lead a campaign against conscription.[20] It was also hoped that the most important cleric resident in Qum, Shaykh Abd al-Karim Ha'iri, might be persuaded to take an active part in the campaign.[21] Isfahani and several of his colleagues, including Ayatullah Mirza Husayn Fishariki, accordingly took up residence in Qum, where they were joined by clerical representatives from Tehran and many provincial towns, including Shiraz, Hamadan, Mashhad and Tabriz, and from Najaf in Iraq. However, Isfahani failed to attract the support of the clerical establishment in Qum, Ha'iri, who had a personal history of political non-involvement, openly declaring his neutrality. Isfahani was further weakened by the fact that the ulama who joined him in Qum were, with one or two exceptions, very minor figures.

The day designated for the first call-up of conscripts in Shiraz was 8 October. On that day the bazaars in Shiraz closed down and remained closed as a protest against conscription, and trade came to a standstill.[22] Similar action was taken in Isfahan and to a lesser extent in Kirmanshah, Qazvin and Tehran. The bazaars in Isfahan and Shiraz, where opposition was most determined, remained closed for three months. The occupational guilds were adamantly opposed to conscription and from 16 October organized in Shiraz and elsewhere a general strike, prevailing upon carpenters, masons, brickmakers and so on to stop work. In Tehran not only were the bazaars closed but there were attempts by crowds to demonstrate in front of the Majlis, although these were prevented by the police. Petitions were presented to the shah but were also of no avail: he gave the cynical reply that as the Majlis had introduced conscription he, as a constitutional monarch, was obliged to give effect to the law.[23]

The government at first responded to these developments with indifference, protests from the southern towns to the capital receiving only the reply that people could continue to keep their businesses closed if they wished, providing there were no disorders. The local authorities, perceiving more clearly the depth of opposition and the gravity of the situation, were more active, launching a propaganda war and attempting to dissuade the protesters from further activity. In Shiraz the governor-general arranged for the Shiraz Majlis deputies to meet a delegation from the opposition on 11 October, on the grounds that it was the Majlis deputies who were responsible for the conscription law. However the Majlis deputies utterly failed to alter the opinions of the delegation, and were indeed rebuffed and humiliated by the encounter. The delegation bluntly denounced both the legitimacy of the Majlis and the regime's perversion of constitutional procedure. The Shirazis told their deputies that they were not genuine representatives of theirs but were nominees of the government and had been forced on them; that there had been no Majlis properly elected by the people since 1916; that according to the constitution five *mujtahid*s must have a place in the Majlis and a voice in its proceedings; and that, since other laws passed by the Majlis were flouted and ignored by the government, as far as they were concerned the conscription law could suffer the same fate.[24]

Martial law was declared in Isfahan and troop reinforcements arrived, but the authorities could make no impact on the solidity of the strikes there and at Shiraz and in Qum. However, in Tehran the agitation against conscription calmed down, though various anonymous leaflets, threatening terrorist action if the law were not modified, reached the shah. The government now showed clear signs of compromise and retreat. On 24 October the shah summoned groups of ulama, merchants and deputies and made them a lengthy speech, the theme of which was his personal devotion to Islam. This heartened the ulama, who regarded it as an admission that he was frightened of religious opinion.[25] The government issued orders to the police and the military to deal leniently with anti-conscription demonstrators in Tehran, and the shah also gave orders for leniency in the carrying out of conscription. On 12 November conscription ceased entirely in Tehran. Furthermore, although out of a total of 3342 called up, 1111 were taken, they were all given a certificate stating that, although they had been conscripted, they would not be called to the colours for the time being.[26] In this way the government hoped to avoid aggravating the crisis while it decided upon a strategy.

Although the shah had been greatly angered by the protests, his acute understanding of political reality and his ready appreciation of political danger indicated the necessity of a tactical retreat, coupled with the appearance of compromise. Early in November he sent his minister of court, Abd ul-Husayn Taymurtash, to Qum to meet the ulama, especially those who had taken refuge there from Isfahan. However, Taymurtash achieved little, the Isfahan ulama declining to see him.[27] It was by now generally believed that the shah was prepared to compromise with the ulama over conscription. Hints were dropped that, although the conscription law would not be annulled, its execution would be carried out very leniently for a number of years; men of military age, though called up yearly, would be allowed to buy exemption; as far as possible, only volunteers would be taken, and if conscripts were necessary they would be taken only from villages. The government was clearly attempting to defuse the opposition of the better-off urban elements, particularly the guilds, without abandoning the central tenets of the conscription policy.

There was little chance of an agreement along these lines. The ulama, firmly established as the leadership of the movement, were motivated not just by dislike of conscription itself but by opposition to the general direction of the regime's reforms and by the steady diminishing of their own power. The opposition of the population in general to conscription was spontaneous, genuine and profound, and aggravated by the corruption of the recruiting commissions, while the more politically aware had wider grievances against the government, the most important being their resentment at the interference of the shah, the military and the government in the elections. Indeed, the view was almost universally held that the Majlis then in session had been elected unconstitutionally. After a month, the closure of the bazaars in Shiraz and Isfahan and the strikes of the guilds were as solid as ever, and constant exhortations were being made to the ulama in other towns to join the movement. Although the big merchants were surreptitiously doing a certain amount of business, those of smaller substance were experiencing genuine distress, while the severe hardship of the apprentices, petty shopkeepers and guildsmen was being alleviated by an arrangement giving them half-pay.[28] The ulama themselves spent a considerable amount of money on sustaining the strike. Some, such as Ayatullah Isfahani himself, were very rich, and Isfahani was personally financing the movement in Isfahan.

Taymurtash's visit to Qum had produced no softening in the attitude of the *basti*s. The ulama in Qum had made no definite statement of their aims, but the situation was becoming increasingly complex, involving a multiplicity of grievances and demands. Although dislike of conscription had originally provoked the protest, there were many other objectives which the ulama now hoped to attain. They hated the new Ministry of Justice and they particularly disliked Taymurtash and his role at court. Most importantly, they wanted the constitution to be respected and the shah to be a constitutional monarch, leaving government to a fully responsible cabinet; they wanted elections to be free and the deputies to be chosen by the people, not the appointees of the shah or the army; and, most crucial of all, they wanted implemented the constitutional provision for a supreme committee of five *mujtahid*s able to scrutinize all bills introduced into the Majlis, to ensure that nothing was done which contravened the shari'ah. So important to them was this last point that they argued that all laws passed by the Majlis in the absence of this committee were in fact unconstitutional and illegal. These opinions were a potent weapon. The ulama were apparently aiming especially at the legislation of the Fifth and current Majlis, and specifically at the Act which deposed the Qajar dynasty, thus threatening the legitimacy of the shah's newly established monarchy.[29]

Meanwhile, the military authorities continued to make a show of implementing conscription. On 16 October the GOC in the south, General Mahmud Khan Ayrum, and the colonel in charge of conscription telegraphed from Isfahan to the press in Shiraz that 517 conscripts and 92 volunteers had been recruited, although the British consul-general in Isfahan noted in his diary that 'some conscripts had presented themselves, but only those who had a valid excuse for not serving'[30], while the appearance of volunteers had been secured by a judicious expenditure of money and the employment of old soldiers in civilian clothes.[31] Finally, after several postponements, all those liable for conscription in Isfahan were ordered to present themselves on 27 November. Of those called up, about 550 were exempted, about 300 presented themselves, and about 500 failed to answer the summons

A settlement

After the failure of Taymurtash's mission to Qum the shah realized that the situation was becoming dangerous. Despite press censorship, news of the strike was being carried throughout the country and its duration began to convey an impression of powerlessness on the part of the central government, and of the decline of the control, civil and military, of the Pahlavi regime. At first the shah continued to insist that amendment of the conscription law rested with the Majlis, while the president of the Majlis, replying to the ulama of Shiraz, and the prime minister, replying to leaders of the merchants, repeated platitudes about leniency in taking conscripts. By early December the shah's impatience for a settlement had become overwhelming. On 10 December he sent the prime minister to Qum, accompanied by Taymurtash and two compliant Tehran clerics. They returned on the 14th, having arrived at an agreement with the ulama. The terms were not immediately announced but the next day the press printed copies of telegrams exchanged between the shah and the ulama. The telegrams were vague but complimentary, and one from the ulama, in which the shah was referred to as the saviour of Iran, had obviously been composed under the influence of Taymurtash himself. Signed by Ayatullah Isfahani as well as Ayatullah Fishariki and two others, it concluded with the hope that by the acts of the only saviour of Iran, Islam and the Muslims would enjoy happiness. The shah's reply stated that he had never had any intention other than to safeguard the glory and greatness of Islam and to preserve all the respect and honour due to the spiritual leaders.[32]

A few days later two of the ulama from Qum came to Tehran, returning with the government's signature to the acceptance of the following five conditions.[33]

1) A revision of the conscription law to be made by the next Majlis.

2) Five high-ranking *mujtahid*s to form a committee to supervise the Majlis, as provided by the constitutional law.

3) Ecclesiastical supervisors for the provincial press to see that nothing anti-Islamic was printed.

4) A strict veto on practices forbidden by Islam, such as drinking of wine, gambling, etc.

5) Reintroduction of the numerous small religious courts for dealing with personal status, the administration of oaths, etc., which had been newly centralized in the Central Court of Justice by the Ministry of Justice.

The government apparently also gave verbal promises concerning other matters, including an undertaking that there would be no government interference in the next elections.

According to the press, these conditions were more or less those on which the truce had been made between Taymurtash and Isfahani; nevertheless the ulama who returned from Tehran with the document bearing the government's signature received a very cold reception in Qum. The *basti*s had expected that their representatives would remain in the capital to see that the government put into immediate effect some at least of the conditions, while the fact that the modification of the conscription law had actually been postponed until the next Majlis was considered very unsatisfactory. It was at first uncertain what line the principal *mujtahid*s gathered in Qum, especially Ayatullah Isfahani, by far the most influential and important, would ultimately adopt, but on 26 December Isfahani, who was nearly ninety and had been unwell for some time, died.[34] This deprived the anti-conscription movement of its leader and also weakened the influence of the remaining ulama over the population in general, making it likely that the truce would become a permanent settlement.

The people of Isfahan and Shiraz had by now become extremely battle-weary, and the onset of winter had further undermined both their resolve and that of the *basti*s in Qum, while they were further demoralized by death of Isfahani at a crucial moment in the negotiations. In fact the bazaars in Isfahan had reopened on 4 December, even before the agreement was formally reached, while the strike ended in Shiraz on 27 December. The crisis was over and the general perception was of a government victory, little prestige having accrued to the ulama. It was true that the government had signed an agreement making certain concessions, but among the general population this was widely considered to be hardly worth the paper on which it was written.

Resistance to conscription was most organized and prolonged in the towns of the south, Isfahan and Shiraz, where leadership was provided by the ulama and the guilds. Elsewhere protests erupted in a more spontaneous way. On 11 December in Rasht, for example, serious anti-conscription riots broke out, led by the women of the town, and the bazaars were closed. The riots resulted in twenty deaths, and martial law was proclaimed, a strict censorship imposed and an armoured car sent from the capital to overawe the population.[35] The government had already decided to exercise great leniency in the recruiting of conscripts and towards the end of 1927 continued at all only for appearances sake. During December in the Tehran districts recruiting was carried out almost secretly and practically on a volunteer basis, while when the commission declared its work complete in Kirmanshah town only fifty recruits had been taken. At the end of the year conscription, which had in any case very slackly been implemented in all the towns throughout the country, and only in the latter months extended to the districts, was temporarily cancelled altogether, and a few volunteers from villages were enlisted at practically the old volunteer rate of pay. From the very beginning the methods employed had allowed of great leakage in manpower and the total number of recruits called up during 1927 probably did not exceed 3000.

For the first six months of 1928 a certain leniency continued in the application of the law. Yet still wherever attempts were made to enforce the law, or even to carry out the registration, a degree of resistance was encountered. For instance, early in January 1928 disturbances occurred in Maraghah, a town in Azarbayjan, in connection with compulsory registration of citizens for recruiting purposes while in Isfahan province a pro-conscription mullah was murdered by Bakhtiyari tribesmen.[36] The work of the recruiting commissions proceeded haltingly and with difficulty, and they concentrated their efforts on the settled peasantry in the villages, who were incapable of the organized, collective and sustained opposition shown by the better-off elements led by the guilds in the towns. During January and February a commission was active in Isfahan province, but no recruits were taken from Isfahan town, only from the villages. During April another attempt was made to apply the law in Isfahan itself, but as a result of the outcry and the closing of the bazaars it was again discontinued. Nevertheless the commission continued its activities in the surrounding villages, apparently collecting few men but a lot of money.[37] By the end of April considerable hardship was being experienced in the villages around Hamadan, although in the town the effect of conscription was practically nil. Again, although by September there were about 800 conscripts undergoing their training in Rasht town, all were from the surrounding villages.

The work of the recruiting commissions was plagued by inefficiency, incompetence and corruption, paradoxically aggravated by the government's decision to implement the policy with leniency. In Rasht town the enrolling of recruits ceased on 7 February. The commission reported to Tehran that of 1158 eligible men, 187 had been enlisted and 557 exempted, while the remainder had not presented themselves for examination. In Kurdistan, when the commission finished their task they had enlisted only about sixty recruits. In the Isfahan area only 40 per cent of those eligible for conscription had even been registered, but the chief conscription officer and his assistant were reported to be making a respectable fortune out of bribes.[38]

New conflicts

Around the middle of 1928 the shah apparently decided the time had come to enforce conscription with renewed determination, and he ordered his divisional commanders to make every effort to make conscription a success. The Ministry of the Interior ordered all provincial governors to give every assistance to the officials responsible for conscription, and an energetic campaign was launched in both the national and the local press in support of conscription as a patriotic duty. By mid-September it was clear that there was increased activity throughout the country in conscripting recruits. However, both the methods employed by the commissions and the results they obtained fell far short of the grandiose expectations of nationalist ideologues, and they also continued to encounter constant opposition. In Kirmanshah, for example, recruiting was very busily carried on but it apparently took the form of seizing domestic servants who could later be 'ransomed'.[39] In early October the bazaars in Shiraz were again closed as a protest against the renewed call-up and there were some casualties as a result of a clash between the troops and demonstrators. In November in Kirman the methods used by the military authorities to obtain recruits caused widespread resentment and there was unrest in the city over both conscription and the enforcement of the new clothing reforms.[40]

In 1928 Tabriz, the provincial capital of Azarbayjan, was the site of the major protest against conscription. Here too, as with the previous year's protests, dislike of conscription meshed with wider resentment at the impact of the imposition of reform to produce an explosive situation and a general challenge to the tightening control of the Tehran regime. By early 1928 nothing had been done to enforce conscription or even registration in Tabriz, a city with a reputation for political radicalism and general toughness. At the end of March the decision was made to enforce registration with drastic measures. For example body-washers and coffin-makers were to be obliged to demand proof of registration from families of deceased persons before providing their services.[41] Yet the authorities still met with little success and at the end of April, apprehensive at the depth of opposition, suspended the application of conscription to Azarbayjan.

When the government extended conscription to Tabriz in 1928, hostility to the government was greatly increased by its decision to enforce simultaneously the wearing of the Pahlavi hat. The unrest thereby generated led to protest meetings being held in mosques and culminated on 17 October in a demonstration by a crowd of about 10,000, which was broken up by the police and the army with some violence.[42] Arrests had begun even before the demonstration took place and continued for some time afterwards. A number of *ulama* were arrested and sent to Tehran, including one of the four *mujtahid*s of Tabriz, Haj Mirza Abu'l Hasan Agha Angaji. Ayatullah Angaji had staunchly opposed the clothing reform, and regarding conscription had advised the population, when faced with the dilemma of having to choose whether to submit to the registration or to abandon their pilgrimages to Mecca, Karbala or Mashhad, to give up their pilgrimages. A number of rich merchants were also arrested. Besides having refused to attend a ceremony in honour of conscription to which they had been invited at the governor-general's palace, they were accused of having given money to the shopkeepers who had closed their shops, and of having provided tea and carpets for the various meetings. In fact, some of these merchants had apparently only acted under considerable popular pressure. Less important people, such as anti-government mullahs of the second rank, faced more serious consequences, being accused of inciting the people to resist the authorities and of treason. Some of them were threatened with hanging, others were immediately flogged.

Through the end of 1928 and into 1929 the military authorities pressed on ruthlessly with conscription. In Tabriz many small shopkeepers, the element who had put up strongest resistance in the bazar, were recruited first.[43] They were often the mainstay of their families, who were left on the verge of starvation. Rampant inefficiency and corruption prevailed everywhere. In Kirmanshah, for example, the dishonesty of the census officials was undisguised, more than one case having occurred in which bearded and wrinkled and obviously middle-aged men were written down as twenty-one, while in Isfahan a colonel of the Census Department who arrived on inspection duty brought to light several cases where bribes were taken for entering false ages. In Shiraz about 10 per cent of those called up were Jews, a proportion far greater than their presence in the general population, and the Kirman conscription committee was reported to be taking every Zoroastrian they could lay their hands on.[44] In Isfahan there were upwards of 60 per cent of absentees and elsewhere there were huge numbers of exemptions. In Gilan, of 550 names examined by the recruiting commission, only 66 were found liable for service. In Hamadan of 300 conscripts called up, only 130 presented themselves, of whom nearly 100 were exempted. Everywhere all those who were actually recruited were drawn from the very poorest sections of the population.

With the crushing of Tabriz, organized resistance to conscription in the towns of Iran was broken. The 'religious–radical alliance',[45] the cooperation between secular reformers and clerical dissidents, which had achieved such success during the constitutional revolution, was in 1920s Iran no longer operative. Indeed, this alliance had been sundered and the two elements put at loggerheads by the ascendancy of Riza Pahlavi and his launch of a modernizing state-building project. The ulama found themselves in opposition to the regime's agenda but without a coherent political and national alternative and were therefore unable to provide sustained leadership to the anti-conscription movement.

Resistance of the tribes

Opposition to conscription then shifted to the rural areas. The peasantry was incapable of sustained and organized resistance, relying instead on escape by flight or, where possessing the means, bribery. The tribes of Iran, however, were both politically more resourceful and more dangerous, still able to mobilize considerable armed strength. Although since 1921 the government had been attempting, with varying degrees of success, to disarm the tribes and bring them under state control, the great tribal confederations of the south, the Bakhtiyari, the Qashqa'i and the Khamsah, and the Kurdish groupings of the west, were far from subdued.

There had never been any reluctance among the tribes to undertake military service. Irregular tribal levies, raised for specific campaigns and officered by tribal khans and chiefs, had indeed been the only significant military resource available to the Iranian state in the nineteenth century and were still, in the late 1920s, of great importance to the fighting capacity of the army. Conscription, however, was viewed with horror.

The absorption of large numbers of young men into a regular army, on the same terms as, and indistinguishable from, peasants and townsmen, their removal from the tribal environment and protection, their subordination to non-tribal authority and the submergence of their tribal identity, was a process which struck at the foundations of tribal existence.

Furthermore, opposition to conscription among the tribes was again embedded in a cluster of grievances and in 1929 a series of armed uprisings broke out in western and southern Iran. In Kurdistan the tribes, fearful of the extension of direct government control in general and in particular of the imposition of conscription and clothing reform, rose in January, drove the army out of the town of Sardasht and besieged the garrison in Saujbulak. Intermittent fighting continued until June, when the government concentrated troops in the Saujbulak area and drove the rebels back to their mountain homes, their leaders taking refuge across the Iraqi border.[46]

The rebellions in southern Iran, though motivated by much the same grievances, were more prolonged and serious.[47] In the early summer of 1929 the Qashqa'i and then the Khamsah broke out into rebellion. Some of the smaller tribes joined in the movement and government authority was threatened throughout the province of Fars. At the beginning of June some sections of the Bakhtiyari in the province of Isfahan also revolted.

Although the army had not yet attempted to call up tribesmen, fear of the future imposition of conscription was one of the principal causes of the uprisings. The tribes were also bitterly opposed to the new dress laws and to the regime's policy of disarmament, and were exasperated after years of harsh treatment and extortion by the military officers placed over them by Riza Shah.[48] The same core demands were put forward by all the rebellious tribes: they were not to be disarmed, and the conscription and dress laws were not to be applied to them. In addition, each tribal group had specific grievances of its own. The Qashqa'i, for example, demanded the release from prison of their hereditary chief, Sawlat al-Dawlah, and his reinstatement as tribal *ilkhani*, while the Kurds insisted that no Persian governor should be appointed in their areas.[49]

The government offered an amnesty to the Qashqa'i, restored Sawlat al-Dawlah, and also adopted a conciliatory approach to the Bakhtiyari, but it did not formally grant the tribesmen's demands. The tribes' ability to offer a sustained challenge to the government was in any case weakened by their own lack of unity and by the end of the summer the uprisings had subsided. Although no tribal conscripts were taken for the time being, the tribal uprisings, like the strikes and protests in Isfahan and Shiraz in 1927, had achieved little but a temporary and apparent concession. They had signally failed to arrest the overall centralizing drive of the regime or to alter the growing disparity between their own power and that of the state. Disarmament of the tribes and the consolidation of Tehran's control continued, followed inexorably as the 1930s progressed by conscription and ultimately forced settlement.

Nevertheless, throughout the 1930s the regime exercised extreme caution when imposing conscription on the tribes, adopting a gradual, piecemeal approach. It was not until the mid-1930s that the first serious and systematic efforts were made to take recruits from the tribes, although from then on the reach of the recruiting commissions was slowly extended, year by year. By the late 1930s, however, conscription had still not been universally applied to the tribes and was still provoking sporadic armed resistance.[50]

Although the shah had been prepared, when this was unavoidable, to temporize with the various elements of opposition, his ultimate determination to force conscription upon the population of Iran was never in doubt, and he had both the requisite political will and the necessary financial resources. In 1931 and 1938 amendments aimed at generally strengthening the conscription law were passed by the Majlis and, organized resistance over, the way was clear for a massive expansion in the army's manpower. The shah initially stated that he wanted an army of 100,000 and indeed the army grew inexorably, from an estimated 37,000 in 1928, to 87,000 in 1935, reaching a massive 127,000 men organized in 18 divisions by 1941, thus actually exceeding the shah's original objectives.

Although conscription certainly produced a large army, it did not produce a strong or efficient army. Despite the huge amounts of money spent annually on the army, the conscripts themselves endured extremely harsh conditions. In 1931 their pay was reduced from an already derisory 7½ qirans to 7 qirans per month (volunteers received 45 qirans per month). Their physique and stamina were reported to be unsatisfactory, they were worked hard in all weathers, poorly fed and housed, and medical and sanitary arrangements were quite inadequate.[51] So bad was the situation that in 1931, on account of the high mortality among troops of the Tehran garrison, special medical officers were appointed by the shah himself as supervisors. The low morale was compounded by a lack of proper training programmes and by the atmosphere of arbitary terror which the shah fostered within the army and which pervaded all ranks from the lowest to the highest. Such an army was naturally of little use on active service, and throughout the 1930s the military authorities continued to raise tribal levies for the small-scale operations which were its only occupation.[52]

Undoubtedly the harsh treatment to which the conscripts were subjected was made easier by the fact that the vast majority were drawn from the very poorest groups in Iranian society. Although the law had theoretically been tightened and occasionally scandals erupted resulting in the punishment of corrupt recruiting officers, bribery and the purchase of exemptions were commonplace and nobody with a few spare tumans needed to 'undergo the unpleasantness of the barrack square'.[53] Indeed, the regime appears to have decided, in the face of the 1927 episode, to use an almost institutionalized system of bribery to defuse the opposition of the better-off.

Conscription transformed the relationship between the army and Iranian society. Its introduction led to an unprecedented intrusion by the military into the lives of ordinary people and to their becoming enmeshed in the institutions of the modernizing state. It was an indispensable and key element in the regime's Persification campaign and in its drive to disseminate the official ideology of secular nationalism with a strong monarchical component. It furthermore provided, for the rural poor who made up the bulk of recruits, a dramatic introduction to modernity in general. Indeed, the army, with its emphasis on uniformity, regularity, discipline, impersonal relationships and 'measured time', may be seen as a quintessentially modern institution, preparing its peasant conscripts for the new demands of industrial capitalism.

Conscription also transformed the character of the Iranian army. It ended the traditional ethnic imbalance in Iranian military formations, the preponderance of the Azari/Turkish element, and ultimately produced an officer corps and rank and file which more accurately reflected the country's ethnic composition. In the short term, however, conscription destroyed what little military effectiveness the army had possessed. The army's fighting strength had always resided in the tribal levies, and their phasing out exposed the more or less complete inadequacy of the poorly trained, badly educated, harshly treated conscripts. Fortunately for the regime, the very pacification of the country which made the imposition of conscription possible also meant an end to the tribal campaigning which had typified the 1920s. The conscript army of the 1930s was a parade-ground army, largely untried in battle and led by complacent and corrupt officers. Like other reforms of the Riza Shah period, conscription resulted in little more than a veneer of modernization. In 1941, when it met its first real test, the Iranian army disintegrated without a struggle: the conscripts simply sold their rifles to the tribes and went home, leaving the whole painful process of rebuilding the army to begin again from scratch. Indeed, the mass desertions of 1941 may perhaps be seen as the most spectacular example of popular resistance to conscription.

Notes

1   For nineteenth-century attempts at military reform, see Stephanie Cronin, *The Army and the Creation of the Pahlavi State in Iran, 1910–1926* (London and New York, 1997), pp. 1–7.

2   The term *'bunichah'* is derived from the word *'bunah'*, in this context meaning an agricultural unit. A. Reza Sheikholeslami, *The Structure of Central Authority in Qajar Iran* (Atlanta, GA, 1997), p. 179.

3   Cronin, *The Army*, pp. 5–6, 120–5.

4   *Ibid.*, pp. 27–9, 56–7. For the Government Gendarmerie, see also Lt.-Col. Parviz Afsar, *Tarikh-i Zhandarmiri-yi Iran* (Qum, 1332); Jahangir Qa'im Maqami, *Tarikh-i Zhandarmiri-yi Iran* (Tehran, 1355). For the Cossack Brigade/Division, see Ahmad Amirahmadi, *Khatirat-i Nakhustin Sipahbud-i Iran* (Tehran, 1373); Amanallah Jahanbani, *Khatirat-i az Dawran-i Darakhshan-i Riza Shah-i Kabir* (Tehran, 1346); F. Kazemzadeh, 'The Origin and Early Development of the Persian Cossack Brigade', *American Slavic and East European Review* 15/3 (October 1956), pp. 351–63.

5   Cronin, *The Army*, passim.

6   *Ibid.*

7   Report on the Organization of the Persian Army, Lt.-Col. H. P. Picot, Durand to Salisbury, 18 January 1900, FO881/7364.

8   Intelligence Summary (hereafter, IS) no. 40, 6 October 1923, FO371/9020/E11740/69/34.

9   IS no. 40, 4 October 1924, FO371/10132E9746/255/34.

10 A translation of the Bill as originally presented to the Majlis in April 1923 may be found in Loraine to Curzon, 28 April 1923, FO371/9021/E5823/71/34.

11 (American) Chargé d'Affaires, W. Smith Murray, to Secretary of State, Washington, 24 March 1925, National Archives Microfilm Publications, Microcopy 715, Roll 12.

12   IS no. 9, 28 February 1925, FO371/10842/E2098/82/34.
13   IS no. 25, 11 December 1926, FO371/12285/E34/34/34.
14   IS no. 1, 8 January 1927, FO371/12285/E512/34/34; IS no. 2, 22 January 1927, FO371/12285/E883/34/34.
15   See, for example, Shahrough Akhavi, *Religion and Politics in Contemporary Iran: Clergy–State Relations in the Pahlavi Period* (New York, 1980).
16   Houchang E. Chehabi, 'Staging the Emperor's New Clothes: dress Codes and Nation-building under Reza Shah', *Iranian Studies* 26, nos. 3–4 (1993), pp. 209–33.
17   IS no. 9, 30 April 1927, FO371/12285/E2318/34/34.
18   IS no. 18, 3 September 1927, FO371/12286/E4109/34/34.
19   The shrine city of Qum, burial place of Fatimah, the sister of the eighth Imam, was an important centre of Shi'ite learning and possessed a tradition of offering *bast* to those in dispute with the temporal authority
20   Husayn Makki, *Tarikh-i Bist Salah-i Iran*, 8 vols. (Tehran, 1323), vol. 4, pp. 415–39.
21   Annual Report 1927, Clive to Chamberlain, 21 May 1928, FO371/13069/E2897/2897/34.
22   Consul Chick, Shiraz, to Clive, 22 October 1927, FO371/12293/E4979/520/34.
23   IS no. 21, 15 October 1927, FO371/12286/E4742/34/34.
24   Consul Chick, Shiraz, to Clive, 22 October 1927.
25   IS no. 22, 29 October 1927, FO371/12286/E4982/34/34.
26   IS no. 24, 26 November 1927, FO371/12286/E5446/34/34.
27   Clive to Chamberlain, 5 November 1927, FO371/12293/E4979/520/34.
28   Consul Chick, Shiraz, to Clive, 8 November 1927, FO371/12293/E5208/520/34.
29   Clive to Chamberlain, 19 November 1927, FO371/12293/E5207/520/34.
30   Quoted in Consul Chick, Shiraz, to Clive, 1 December 1927, FO371/13056/E40/40/34.
31   IS no. 22, 29 October 1927.
32   Translations in Consul Chick, Shiraz, to Clive, 1 December 1927.
33   Clive to Chamberlain, 29 December 1927, FO371/13056/E375/40/34.
34   Isfahani's death immediately gave rise to rumours that he had been poisoned on the orders of the Tehran authorities. Since he was aged and unwell, he may well have died of natural causes, although the shah's regime was certainly developing a habit of secretly murdering its opponents.
35   IS no. 26, 24 December 1927, FO371/13055/E584/38/34.
36   IS no. 2, 21 January 1928, FO371/13055/E722/38/34; IS no. 4, 18 February 1928, FO371/13055/E1301/38/34.
37   IS no. 9, 28 April 1928, FO371/13055/E2673/38/34.
38   IS no. 6, 17 March 1928, FO371/13055/E2129/38/34.

39 IS no. 18, 1 September 1928, FO371/13055/E4673/38/34.

40 IS no. 21, 13 October 1928, FO371/13055/E5275/38/34; IS no. 23, 17 November 1928, FO371/13055/E5970/38/34. On 28 December the Majlis passed the Uniform Dress Law, which stated that the official clothing for Iranian men was the hat and suit, and outlawed other forms of dress. See Chehabi, 'Staging the emperor's new clothes'.

41 IS no. 7, 31 March 1928, FO371/13055/E2135/38/34.

42 Consul Gilliat-Smith, Tabriz, to Parr, 19 October 1928, FO371/13056/E5211/40/34.

43 Extract from Tabriz Consulate Diary, no. 11, November 1928, Clive to Chamberlain, 12 December 1928, FO371/13781/E95/95/34.

44 IS no. 2, 19 January 1929, FO371/13784/E1004/34; IS no. 23, 16 November 1929, FO371/13785/E6248/104/34.

45 For an analysis of this concept see the pioneering work of Nikki Keddie, for example 'The Origins of the Religious–Radical Alliance in Iran', in Nikki R. Keddie, *Iran: Religion, Politics and Society* (London, 1980), pp. 53–65.

46 Consul Gilliat-Smith, Tabriz, to Clive, 6 June 1929, FO371/13781/E3351/95/34; Annual Report 1929, Clive to Henderson, 30 April 1930, FO371/14543/E2445/522/34.

47 For these rebellions see Kavih Bayat, *Shurish-i 'Asha'ir-i Fars* (Tehran, 1372); Ja'afar Quli Khan Amir-i Bahadur, *Khatirat-i Sardar-i As'ad Bakhtiyari* (Tehran, 1372), pp. 231–2.

48 Annual Report 1929.

49 Consul Gilliat-Smith, Tabriz, to Clive, 6 June 1929; Annual Report 1929.

50 The rising of the Kurdish tribes in the Sardasht area in the spring of 1939, for example, was partly a result of the call for conscripts. IS no. 7, 8 April 1939, FO371/23261/E3024/216/34.

51 Annual Report 1931, Hoare to Simon, 12 June 1932, FO371/16077/E3354/3354/34.

52 See, for example, Annual Report 1936, Seymour to Eden, 30 January 1937, FO371/20836/E1435/1435/34

53 Annual Report 1930, Clive to Henderson, 22 May 1931, FO371/15356/E3067/3067/34.

Notes on Contributors

Virginia Aksan is associate professor in the Department of History of McMaster University, Hamilton, Ontario.

Stephanie Cronin is a researcher attached to the School of Oriental and African Studies, University of London.

Dick Douwes is academic coordinator of the International Institute for the Study of Islam in the Modern World in Leiden.

Khaled Fahmy is associate professor at the Near Eastern Studies Department of Princeton University.

Sergei Kudryashev is editor of the historical journal *Rodina* in Moscow.

Jan Lucassen is head of the research department of the International Institute of Social History in Amsterdam (IISH), and also holds a private chair of social history in the Free University, Amsterdam.

Odile Moreau has recently completed a PhD thesis, on the working of the Ottoman General Staff, at the University of Paris.

Nicole van Os is a PhD student at Nijmegen University, and also works as a representative in Istanbul in the Turkish Studies Department of Leiden University.

Daniel Panzac is senior research fellow at the Institut de Recherches et d'Etudes sur le Monde Arabe at Musulman of the University of Aix-Marseille.

Erik Jan Zürcher holds the chair of Turkish Studies at Leiden University, and is a senior research fellow at the IISH, Amsterdam.